T0116526

DOOMCRUSHER

SWORD OF VICTORY

JUSTIN M BOLSTER

WESTBOW
PRESS®
A DIVISION OF THOMAS NELSON
& ZONDERVAN

WestBow Press books may be ordered through booksellers or by contacting:

WestBow Press
A Division of Thomas Nelson & Zondervan
1663 Liberty Drive
Bloomington, IN 47403
www.westbowpress.com
844-714-3454

ISBN: 979-8-3850-0802-5 (sc)
ISBN: 979-8-3850-0803-2 (e)

Library of Congress Control Number: 2023917985

Print information available on the last page.

WestBow Press rev. date: 09/26/2023

DOOMCRUSHER
THE SWORD OF VICTORY

The weapon created from the New Testament

The darkness is passing away, and the true light is already shining

Guard your heart and mind with these words. This book was made to be a great tool when facing adversity and to equip you to overcome darkness by His word. Made to be a rock, it is a collection of powerful scripture to help you live strong every day and have victory in Christ. DOOMCRUSHER was designed to protect you and to give you peace and life. The truth in this book gave me the ability to stay in the Spirit and was a weapon of hope in hard times. This book will protect you from anything that could oppress you and will set you free. Ask for understanding in all things. May this book guard your heart and be a source of power and strength in your spirit!! Peace always!! - Jus

THE EDGE OF THE SWORD

COLLECTION OF GREAT AND POWERFUL SCRIPTURE

"We are pressed on every side by troubles, but we are not crushed and broken. We are perplexed, but we don't give up and quit. We are hunted down, but God never abandons us. We get knocked down, but we get up again and keep going." 2 CORINTHIANS 4:8-9 from THE MESSAGE by Eugene H. Peterson

Luke

**"He said to him, "What is written in the law? What is your reading of it?" So, he answered and said, "You shall love the Lord your God with all your heart, with all your soul, and with all your strength, and with all your mind, and love your neighbor as yourself." And He said to him," You have answered rightly; do this and you will live." 10:26 NKJV (New King James Translation)

**"And I tell you, ask, and it will be given to you; seek, and you will find; knock, and it will be opened to you. For everyone who asks receives, and the one who seeks finds, and to the one who knocks it will be opened." 11:9 ESV (English Standard Translation)

**"So, I say to you, ask, and it will be given to you; seek, and you will find; knock, and it will be opened to you. For everyone who asks receives, and he who seeks finds, and to him who knocks it will be opened." 11:9 NKJV

**"nor will they say, 'See here!' or 'See there!' For indeed, the kingdom of God is within you." 17:21 NKJV

**"Then He spoke a parable to them, that men always ought to pray and not lose heart." 18:1 NKJV

John

**"In Him was life, and the life was the light of men. The light shines in the darkness, and the darkness has not overcome it." 1:4 ESV

**"In Him was life, and the life was the light of men. And the light shines in the darkness, and the darkness did not comprehend it." 1:4 NKJV

**"I have come into the world as light, so that whoever believes in Me may not remain in darkness. If anyone hears My words and does not keep them, I do not judge him; for I did not come to judge the world but to save the world." 12:46 ESV

**"I have come as a light into the world, that whoever believes in Me should not abide in darkness. And if anyone hears My words and does not believe, I do not judge him; for I did not come to judge the world but to save the world." 12:46 NKJV

**"You call Me Teacher and Lord, and you are right, for so I am. If I then, your Lord and Teacher, have washed your feet, you also ought to wash one another's feet. For I have given you an example, that you also should do just as I have done to you." 13:13 ESV

**"You call Me Teacher and Lord, and you say well, for so I am. If I then, your Lord and Teacher, have washed your feet, you also ought to wash one another's feet. For I have given you and example, that you should do as I have done to you." 13:13 NKJV

**"A new commandment I give to you, that you love one another: just as I have loved you, you also are to love one another. By this all people will know that you are My disciples, if you have love for one another." 13:34 ESV

**"A new commandment I give to you, that you love one another; as I have loved you, that you also love one another. By this all will know that you are My disciples, if you have love for one another." 13:34 NKJV

**"Every branch in Me that does not bear fruit He takes away, and every branch that does bear fruit He prunes, that it may bear more fruit. Already you are clean because of the word that I have spoken to you. Abide in Me, and I in you. As the branch cannot bear fruit by itself, unless it abides in the vine, neither can you, unless you abide in Me." 15:2 ESV

**"Every branch in Me that does not bear fruit He takes away; and every branch that bears fruit He prunes, that it may bear more fruit. You are already clean because of the word which I have spoken to you. Abide in Me, and I in you. As the branch cannot bear fruit of itself, unless it abides in the vine, neither can you, unless you abide in Me." 15:2 NKJV

**"I have said these things to you, that in Me you may have peace. In the world you will have tribulation. But take heart; I have overcome the world." 16:33 ESV

**"These things I have spoken to you, that in Me you may have peace. In the world you will have tribulation; but be of good cheer, I have overcome the world." 16:33 NKJV

**"As You sent Me into the world, so I have sent them into the world." 17:18 ESV

Acts

**"For David says concerning Him, "I saw the Lord always before me, for He is at my right hand that I may not be shaken; therefore my heart was glad, and my tongue rejoiced; my flesh also will dwell in hope. For You will not abandon my soul to Hades, or let your holy one see corruption. You have made known to me the paths of life; you will make me full of gladness with Your presence." 2:25 ESV

**"strengthening the souls of the disciples, encouraging them to continue in the faith, and saying that through many tribulations we must enter the kingdom of God." 14:22 ESV

**"strengthening the souls of the disciples, exhorting them to continue in the faith, and saying, "We must through many tribulations enter the kingdom of God." 14:22 NKJV

Romans

**"Therefore, since we have been justified by faith, we have peace with God through our Lord Jesus Christ. Through Him we have also obtained access by faith into this grace in which we stand, and we rejoice in hope of the glory of God. Not only that, but we rejoice in our sufferings, knowing that suffering produces endurance, and endurance produces character, and character produces hope, and hope does not put us to shame, because God's love has been poured into our hearts through the Holy Spirit who has been given to us. For while we were still weak, at the right time Christ died for the ungodly." 5:1 ESV

**"Therefore, having been justified by faith, we have peace with God through our Lord Jesus Christ, through whom also we have access by faith into this grace in which we stand, and rejoice in hope of the glory of God. And not only that, but we also glory in tribulations, knowing that tribulation produces perseverance, and perseverance, character, and character, hope. Now hope does not disappoint, because the love of God has been poured out in our hearts by the Holy Spirit who was given to us. For when we were still without strength, in due time Christ died for the ungodly." 5:1 NKJV

**"For the death He died He died to sin, once for all, but the life He lives He lives to God. So, you also must consider yourselves dead to sin and alive to God in Christ Jesus." 6:10 ESV

**"For the death that He died, He died to sin once for all; but the life that He lives, He lives to God. Likewise, you also, reckon yourselves to be dead indeed to sin, but alive to God in Christ Jesus our Lord. Therefore, do not let sin reign in your mortal body, that you should obey it in its lusts. And do not present your members as instruments of unrighteousness to sin but present yourselves to God as being alive from the dead, and your members as instruments of righteousness to God. For sin shall not have dominion over you, for you are not under law but under grace." 6:10 NKJV

**"For to set the mind on the flesh is death, but to set the mind on the Spirit is life and peace." 8:6 ESV

**"Let love be without hypocrisy. Abhor what is evil. Cling to what is good. Be kindly affectionate to one another with brotherly love, in honor giving preference to one another." 12:9 NKJV

**"The God of peace will soon crush Satan under your feet. The grace of our Lord Jesus Christ be with you." 16:20 ESV

**"And the god of peace will crush Satan under your feet shortly." 16:20 NKJV

1 Corinthians

**"Be watchful, stand firm in the faith, act like men, be strong. Let all that you do be done in love." 16:13 ESV

**"Watch, stand fast in the faith, be brave, be strong. Let all that you do be done with love." 16:13 NKJV

2 Corinthians

**"Indeed, we felt that we had received the sentence of death. But that was to make us rely not on ourselves but on God who raises the dead." 1:9 ESV

**"Yes, we had the sentence of death in ourselves, that we should not trust in ourselves but in God who raises the dead, who delivered us from so great a death, and does deliver us; in whom we trust that He will still deliver us." 1:9 NKJV

**"But He said to me, "My grace is sufficient for you, for my power is made perfect in weakness. "Therefore, I will boast even more gladly of my weaknesses, so that the power of Christ may rest upon me. For the sake of Christ, then, I am content with weaknesses, insults, hardships, persecutions, and calamities. For when I am weak, then I am strong." 12:9 ESV

**"And He said to me, "My grace is sufficient for you, for My strength is made perfect in weakness." Therefore, most gladly I will rather boast in my infirmities, that the power of Christ may rest upon me. Therefore, I take pleasure in infirmities, in reproaches, in needs, in persecutions, in distresses, for Christ's sake. For when I am weak, then I am strong." 12:9 NKJV

Galatians

**"I have been crucified with Christ. It is no longer I who live, but Christ who lives in me." 2:20 ESV

**"I have been crucified with Christ; it is no longer I who live, but Christ lives in me; and the life which I now live in the flesh I live by faith in the Son of God, who loved me and gave Himself for me." 2:20 NKJV

**"For freedom Christ has set us free; stand firm therefore, and do not submit again to a yoke of slavery." 5:1 ESV

**"Stand fast therefore in the liberty by which Christ has made us free, and do not be entangled again with a yoke of bondage." 5:1 NKJV

**"But the fruit of the Spirit is love, joy, peace, patience, kindness, goodness, faithfulness, gentleness, self-control; against such things there is no law. And those who belong to Christ Jesus have crucified the flesh with its passions and desires." 5:22 ESV

**"But the fruit of the Spirit is love, joy, peace, longsuffering, kindness, goodness, faithfulness, gentleness, self-control. Against such there is no law. And those who are Christ's have crucified the flesh with its passions and desires." 5:22 NKJV

**"Do not be deceived: for whatever one sows, that will he also reap. For the one who sows to his own flesh will from the flesh reap corruption, but the one who sows to the Spirit will from the Spirit reap eternal life. And let us not grow weary of doing good, for in due season we will reap, if we do not give up." 6:7 ESV

**"Do not be deceived; for whatever a man sows, that he will also reap. For he who sows to his flesh will of the flesh reap corruption, but he who sows to the Spirit will of the Spirit reap everlasting life. And let us not grow weary while doing good, for in due season we shall reap if we do not lose heart." 6:7 NKJV

Ephesians

**"that according to the riches of his glory He may grant you to be strengthened with power through His Spirit in your inner being, so that Christ may dwell in your hearts through faith- that you, being rooted and grounded in love, may have strength to comprehend with all the saints what is the breadth and length and height and depth, and to know the love of Christ that surpasses knowledge, that you may be filled with all the fullness of God." 3:16 ESV

**"walk in a manner worthy of the calling to which you have been called, with all humility and gentleness, with patience, bearing with one another in love, eager to maintain the unity of the Spirit in the bond of peace." 4:1 ESV

**"walk worthy of the calling with which you were called, with all lowliness and gentleness, with longsuffering, bearing with one another in love, endeavoring to keep the unity of the Spirit in the bond of peace." 4:1 NKJV

**"and to be renewed in the spirit of your minds, and to put on the new self, created after the likeness of God in true righteousness and holiness." 4:23 ESV

**"be renewed in the spirit of your mind, and that you put on the new man which was created according to God, in true righteousness and holiness." 4:23 NKJV

**"Let no corrupting talk come out of your mouths, but only such as is good for building up, as fits the occasion, that it may give grace to those who hear." 4:29 ESV

**"Let no corrupt word proceed out of your mouth, but what is good for necessary edification, that it may impart grace to the hearers." 4:29 NKJV

**"Finally, be strong in the Lord and in the strength of His might. Put on the whole armor of God, that you may be able to stand against the schemes of the devil. For we do not wrestle against flesh and blood, but against the rulers, against the authorities, against the cosmic powers over this present darkness, against the spiritual forces of evil in the heavenly places." 6:10 ESV

**"Finally, my brethren, be strong in the Lord and in the power of His might. Put on the whole armor of God, that you may be able to stand against the wiles of the devil. For we do not wrestle against flesh and blood, but against principalities, against powers, against the rulers of the darkness of this age, against spiritual hosts of wickedness in the heavenly places. Therefore, take up the whole armor of God, that you may be able to withstand in the evil day, and having done all, to stand." 6:10 NKJV

**"Stand therefore, having fastened on the belt of truth. And having put on the breastplate of righteousness, and, as shoes for your feet, having put on the readiness given by the gospel of peace. In all circumstances take up the shield of faith, with which you can extinguish all the flaming darts of the evil one; and take the helmet of salvation, and the sword of the Spirit, which is the word of God, praying at all times in the Spirit, with all prayer and supplication. To that end keep alert with all perseverance, making supplication for all the saints." 6:14 ESV

Philippians

**"And I am sure of this, that He who began a good work in you will bring it to completion at the day of Jesus Christ." 1:6 ESV

**"being confident of this very thing, that He who has begun a good work in you will complete it until the day of Jesus Christ." 1:6 NKJV

**"Do nothing from selfish ambition or conceit, but in humility count others more significant than yourselves. Let each of you look not only to his own interests, but also to the interests of others. Have this mind among yourselves, which is yours in Christ Jesus, who, though He was in the form of God, did not count equality with God a thing to be grasped, but emptied Himself, by taking the form of a servant." 2:3 ESV

**"Do all things without grumbling or disputing, that you may be blameless and innocent, children of God without blemish in the midst of a crooked and twisted generation, among whom you shine as lights in the world, holding fast to the word of life, so that in the day of Christ I may be proud that I did not run in vain or labor in vain." 2:14 ESV

**"Do all things without complaining and disputing, that you may become blameless and harmless, children of God without fault in the midst of a crooked and perverse generation, among whom you shine as lights in the world, holding fast the word of life, so that I may rejoice in the day of Christ that I have not run in vain or labored in vain." 2:14 NKJV

**"Not that I have already obtained this or am already perfect, but I press on to make it my own, because Christ Jesus has made me His own... But one thing I do: forgetting what lies behind and straining forward to what lies ahead, I press on toward the goal for the prize of the upward call of God in Christ Jesus." 3:12 ESV

**"Not that I have already attained, or am already perfected; but I press on, that I may lay hold of that for which Christ Jesus has also laid hold of me. Brethren, I do not count myself to have apprehended; but one thing I do, forgetting those things which are behind and reaching forward to those things which are ahead, I press toward the goal for the prize of the upward call of God in Christ Jesus." 3:12 NKJV

**"Rejoice in the Lord always; again, I will say, rejoice. Let your reasonableness be known to everyone. The Lord is at hand; do not be anxious about anything, but in everything by prayer and supplication with thanksgiving let your requests be made known to God. And the peace of God, which surpasses all understanding, will guard your hearts and your minds in Christ Jesus. Finally, brothers, whatever is true, whatever is honorable, whatever is just, whatever is pure, whatever is lovely, whatever is commendable, if there is any excellence, if there is anything worthy of praise, think about these things. What you have learned and received and heard and seen in me- practice these things, and the God of peace will be with you." 4:4 ESV

**"I can do all things through Him who strengthens me." 4:13 ESV

**"I can do all things through Christ who strengthens me." 4:13 NKJV

Colossians

**"so as to walk in a manner worthy of the Lord, fully pleasing to Him, bearing fruit in every good work and increasing in the knowledge of God. May you be strengthened with all power, according to His glorious might, for all endurance and patience with joy, giving thanks to the Father, who has qualified you to share in the inheritance of the saints in light." 1:10 ESV

**"that you may walk worthy of the Lord, fully pleasing Him, being fruitful in every good work and increasing in the knowledge of God; strengthened with all might, according to His glorious power, for all patience and longsuffering with joy; giving thanks to the Father who has qualified us to be partakers of the inheritance of the saints in the light. He has delivered us from the power of darkness and conveyed us into the kingdom of the Son of His love, in whom we have redemption through His blood, the forgiveness of sins." 1:10 NKJV

**"Therefore, as you received Christ Jesus the Lord, so walk in Him, rooted and built up in Him and established in the faith, just as you were taught, abounding in thanksgiving." 2:6 ESV

**"As you therefore have received Christ Jesus the Lord, so walk in Him, rooted and built up in Him and established in the faith, as you have been taught, abounding in it with thanksgiving. Beware lest anyone cheat you through philosophy and empty deceit, according to the tradition of men, according to the basic principles of the world, and not according to Christ. For in Him dwells all the fullness of the Godhead bodily; and you are complete in Him, who is the head of all principality and power." 2:6 NKJV

**"Put on then, as God's chosen ones, holy and beloved, compassionate hearts, kindness, humility, meekness, and patience, bearing with one another and, if one has a complaint against another, forgiving each other; as the Lord has forgiven you, so you also must forgive. And above all these put-on love, which binds everything together in perfect harmony." 3:12 ESV

**"Therefore, as the elect of God, holy and beloved, put on tender mercies, kindness, humility, meekness, longsuffering; bearing with one another, and forgiving one another, if anyone has a complaint against another; even as Christ forgave you, so you also must do. But above all these things put on love, which is the bond of perfection. And let the peace of God rule in your hearts, to which also you were called in one body; and be thankful. Let the word of Christ dwell in you richly in all wisdom, teaching and admonishing one another." 3:12 NKJV

1 Thessalonians

**"But since we belong to the day, let us be sober, having put on the breastplate of faith and love, and for a helmet the hope of salvation. For God has not destined us for wrath, but to obtain salvation through our Lord Jesus Christ, who died for us so that whether we are awake or sleep we might live with Him. Therefore encourage one another and build one another up." 5:8 ESV

**"And we urge you, brothers, admonish the idle, encourage the fainthearted, help the weak, be patient with them all." 5:14 ESV

**"Now we exhort you, brethren, warn those who are unruly, comfort the fainthearted, uphold the weak, be patient with all. See that no one renders evil for evil to anyone, but always pursue what is good both for yourselves and for all. Rejoice always, pray without ceasing, in everything give thanks; for this is the will of God in Christ Jesus for you." 5:14 NKJV

2 Thessalonians

**"not to be quickly shaken in mind or alarmed, either by a spirit or a spoken word, or a letter seeming to be from us, to the effect that the day of the Lord has come." 2:2 ESV

**"May the Lord direct your hearts to the love of God and to the steadfastness of Christ." 3:5 ESV

**"Now may the Lord direct your hearts into the love of God and into the patience of Christ." 3:5 NKJV

1 Timothy

**"The aim of our charge is love that issues from a pure heart and a good conscience and a sincere faith." 1:5 ESV

**"... teach no other doctrine, nor give heed to fables and endless genealogies, which cause disputes rather than godly edification which is in faith. Now the purpose of the commandment is love from a pure heart, from a good conscience, and from sincere faith." 1:3 NKJV

**"But as for you, O man of God, flee these things. Pursue righteousness, godliness, faith, love, steadfastness, gentleness. Fight the good fight of the faith. Take hold of the eternal life to which you were called and about which you made the good confession in the presence of many witnesses." 6:11 ESV

**"But you, O man of God, flee these things and pursue righteousness, godliness, faith, love, patience, gentleness. Fight the good fight of faith, lay hold on eternal life, to which you were also called and have confessed the good confession in the presence of many witnesses. I urge you in the sight of God who gives life to all things, and before Christ Jesus who witnessed the good confession before Pontius Pilate, that you keep the commandment without spot, blameless until our Lord Jesus Christ's appearing." 6:11 NKJV

2 Timothy

**"You therefore my son, be strong in the grace that is in Christ Jesus." 2:1 NKJV

**"Share in suffering as a good soldier of Christ Jesus. No soldier gets entangled in civilian pursuits, since his aim is to please the one who enlisted him. An athlete is not crowned unless he competes according to the rules. It is the hard-working farmer who ought to have the first share of the crops. Think over what I say, for the Lord will give you understanding in everything." 2:3 ESV

**"You therefore must endure hardship as a good soldier of Jesus Christ. No one engaged in warfare entangles himself with the affairs of this life, that he may please the one who enlisted him as a soldier. And, if anyone competes in athletics, he is not crowned unless he competes according to the rules." 2:3 NKJV

**"Do your best to present yourself to God as one approved, a worker who has no need to be ashamed, rightly handling the word of truth." 2:15 ESV

**"Be diligent to present yourself approved to God, a worker who does not need to be ashamed, rightly dividing the word of truth. But shun profane and idle babblings, for they will increase to more ungodliness." 2:15 NKJV

Hebrews

**"Long ago, at many times and in many ways, God spoke to our fathers by the prophets, but in these last days He has spoken to us by His Son, whom He appointed the heir of all things, through whom also He created the world. He is the radiance of the glory of God and the exact imprint of His nature, and He upholds the universe by the word of His power." 1:1 ESV

**"has in these last days spoken to us by His Son, whom He has appointed heir of all things, through whom also He made the worlds; who being the brightness of His glory and the express image of His person, and upholding all things by the word of His power, when He had by Himself purged our sins, sat down at the right hand of the majesty on high." 1:2 NKJV

**"For this is the covenant that I will make with the house of Israel after those days, declares the Lord: I will put My laws into their minds, and write them on their hearts, and I will be their God, and they shall be my people. And they shall not teach, each one his neighbor and each one his brother, saying, 'Know the Lord,' for they shall all know Me, from the least of them to the greatest. For I will be merciful toward their iniquities, and I will remember their sins no more." 8:10 ESV

**"And have you forgotten the exhortation that addresses you as sons? My son, do not regard lightly the discipline of the Lord, nor be weary when reproved by Him. For the Lord disciplines the one He loves, and chastises every son whom He receives." 12:5 ESV

**"And you have forgotten the exhortation which speaks to you as to sons: My son, do not despise the chastening of the Lord, Nor be discouraged when you are rebuked by Him; For whom the Lord loves He chastens, and scourges every son whom He receives." 12:5 NKJV

**"For the moment all discipline seems painful rather than pleasant, but later it yields the peaceful fruit of righteousness to those who have been trained by it." 12:11 ESV

**"Now no chastening seems to be joyful for the present, but painful; nevertheless, afterward it yields the peaceable fruit of righteousness to those who have been trained by it." 12:11 NKJV

James

**"If you really fulfill the royal law according to the scripture, "You shall love your neighbor as yourself," you are doing well." 2:8 ESV

**"For we all stumble in many ways. And if anyone does not stumble in what he says, he is a perfect man, able also to bridle his whole body." 3:2 ESV

**"For we all stumble in many things. If anyone does not stumble in word, he is a perfect man, able also to bridle the whole body." 3:2 NKJV

**"Submit yourselves therefore to God. Resist the devil, and he will flee from you. Draw near to God and He will draw near to you. Cleanse your hands, you sinners, and purify your hearts." 4:7 ESV

1 Peter

**"Therefore, preparing your minds for action, and being sober-minded, set your hope fully on the grace that will be brought to you at the revelation of Jesus Christ. As obedient children, do not be conformed to the passions of your former ignorance, but as He who called you is holy, you also be holy in your conduct." 1:13 ESV

**"Therefore gird up the loins of your mind, be sober, and rest your hope fully on the grace that is to be brought to you at the revelation of Jesus Christ; as obedient children, not conforming yourselves to the former lusts, as in your ignorance; but as He who called you is holy, you also be holy in all your conduct." 1:13 NKJV

**"When He was reviled, he did not revile in return; when He suffered, He did not threaten, but continued entrusting Himself to Him who judges justly. He Himself bore our sins in His body on the tree, that we might die to sin and live to righteousness. By His wounds you have been healed. For you were straying like sheep, but have now returned to the Shepherd and Overseer of your souls." 2:23 ESV

**"For to this you were called, because Christ also suffered for us, leaving us an example, that you should follow His steps: "Who committed no sin, Nor was deceit found in His mouth"; who, when He was reviled, did not revile in return; when He suffered, He did not threaten, but committed Himself to Him you judges righteously; who Himself bore our sins in His own body on the tree, that we, having died to sins, might live for righteousness- by whose stripes you were healed. For you were like sheep going astray, but have now returned to the Shepherd and Overseer of your souls." 2:21 NKJV

**"Now who is there to harm you if you are zealous for what is good? But even if you should suffer for righteousness sake, you will be blessed. Have no fear of them, nor be troubled, but in your hearts honor Christ the Lord as holy, always being prepared to make a defense to anyone who asks you for a reason for the hope that is in you; yet do it with gentleness and respect, having a good conscience." 3:13 ESV

***"And who is he who will harm you if you become followers of what is good? But even if you should suffer for righteousness' sake, you are blessed. And do not be afraid of their threats, nor be troubled. But sanctify the Lord God in your hearts, and always be ready to give a defense to everyone who asks you for a reason for the hope that is in you, with meekness and fear; having a good conscience." 3:13 NKJV

2 Peter

***"... make every effort to supplement your faith with virtue, and virtue with knowledge, and knowledge with self-control, and self-control with steadfastness, and steadfastness with godliness, and godliness with brotherly affection, and brotherly affection with love. For if these qualities are yours and are increasing, they keep you from being ineffective or unfruitful in the knowledge of our Lord Jesus Christ." 1:5 ESV

***"... giving all diligence, add to your faith virtue, to virtue knowledge, to knowledge self-control, to self-control perseverance, to perseverance godliness, to godliness brotherly kindness, to brotherly kindness love. For if these things are yours and abound, you will be neither barren nor unfruitful in the knowledge of our Lord Jesus Christ." 1:5 NKJV

1 John

***"Whoever loves his brother abides in the light, and in him there is no cause for stumbling." 2:10 ESV

***"He who loves his brother abides in the light, and there is no cause for stumbling in him." 2:10 NKJV

***"And everyone who thus hopes in Him purifies himself as he is pure." 3:3 ESV

***"By this we know love, that He laid down His life for us, and we ought to lay down our lives for the brothers. But if anyone has the world's goods and sees his brother in need, yet closes his heart against him, how does God's love abide in him? Little children, let us not love in word or talk but in deed and truth. By this we shall know that we are of the truth and reassure our heart before Him; for whenever our heart condemns us, God is greater than our heart, and He knows everything. Beloved, if our heart does not condemn us, we have confidence before God; and whatever we ask we receive from Him, because we keep His commandments and do what pleases Him. And this is His commandment, that we believe in the name of His Son Jesus Christ and love one another, just as He has commanded us. Whoever keeps His commandments abides in God, and God in him. And by this we know that He abides in us, by the Spirit whom He has given us." 3:16 ESV

DOOMCRUSHER

Matthew

*"Even now the axe is laid to the root of the trees. Every tree therefore that does not bear good fruit is cut down and thrown into the fire." 3:10 ESV

"Therefore, every tree which does not bear good fruit is cut down and thrown into the fire." 3:10 NKJV

*"...the people dwelling in darkness have seen a great light, and for those dwelling in the region and shadow of death, on them a light has dawned. From that time Jesus began to preach, saying, "Repent, for the kingdom of heaven is at hand."" 4:16 ESV

"The people who sat in darkness have seen a great light, and upon those who sat in the region and shadow of death light has dawned. From that time Jesus began to preach and say, "Repent, for the kingdom of heaven is at hand." 4:16 NKJV

-Helps me to understand the condition of the world and how great the love and power of our Savior is.

*"Blessed are the poor in spirit, for theirs is the kingdom of heaven. Blessed are those who mourn, for they shall be comforted. Blessed are the meek, for they shall inherit the earth. Blessed are those who hunger and thirst for righteousness, for they shall be satisfied. Blessed are the merciful, for they shall receive mercy. Blessed are the pure in heart, for they shall see God. Blessed are the peacemakers, for they shall be called sons of God. Blessed are those who are persecuted for righteousness' sake, for theirs is the kingdom of heaven. Blessed are you when others revile

you and persecute you and utter all kinds of evil against you falsely on my account. Rejoice and be glad, for your reward is great in heaven, for so they persecuted the prophets who were before you." 5:3 ESV

"Blessed are the poor in spirit, for theirs is the kingdom of heaven. Blessed are those who mourn, for they shall be comforted. Blessed are the meek, for they shall inherit the earth. Blessed are those who hunger and thirst for righteousness, for they shall be filled. Blessed are the merciful, for they shall obtain mercy. Blessed are the pure in heart, for they shall see God. Blessed are the peacemakers, for they shall be called sons of God. Blessed are those who are persecuted for righteousness sake, for theirs is the kingdom of heaven. Blessed are you when they revile and persecute you, and say all kinds of evil against you falsely for My sake. Rejoice and be exceedingly glad, for great is your reward in heaven, for so they persecuted the prophets who were before you." 5:3 NKJV

-This knowledge has given me great hope and truth that is awesomely powerful.

*"You are the light of the world. A city set on a hill cannot be hidden. Nor do people light a lamp and put it under a basket, but on a stand, and it gives light to all in the house. In the same way, let your light shine before others, so that they may see your good works and give glory to your Father who is in heaven." 5:14 ESV

"You are the light of the world. A city that is set on a hill cannot be hidden. Nor do they light a lamp and put it under a basket, but on a lampstand, and it gives light to all who are in the house. Let your light so shine before men, that they may see your good works and glorify your Father in heaven. 5:14 NKJV

-Jesus wants us to stand out and be light for all people! You will face adversity but choose to react and face it with courage. Be all you can be, have confidence in yourself and peace in your heart. Only God's opinion matters.

*"Let what you say be simply 'Yes' or 'No'; anything more than this comes from evil." 5:37 ESV

"But let your 'Yes' be 'Yes', and your 'No,' 'No.' For whatever is more than these is from the evil one." 5:37 NKJV

-It's always prudent to not speak when it does no good. Your words can totally change the world around you. Speak love and life. Let your words be seasoned with salt, make peace.

*"You have heard that it was said, 'You shall love your neighbor and hate your enemy.' But I say to you, love your enemies and pray for those who persecute you." 5:43 ESV

"You have heard that it was said, 'You shall love your neighbor and hate your enemy. But I say to you, love your enemies, bless those who curse you, do good to those who hate you, and pray for those who spitefully use you and persecute you, that you may be sons of your Father in heaven" 5:43 NKJV

-This helps me to understand the heart of God and his compassion and my purpose.

*"Thus, when you give to the needy, sound no trumpet before you, as the hypocrites do in the synagogues and in the streets." 6:2 ESV

"Therefore, when you do a charitable deed, do not sound a trumpet before you as the hypocrites do in the synagogues and in the streets, that they may have glory from men. ..But when you do a charitable deed, do not let your left hand know what your right hand is doing, that your charitable deed may be in secret; and your Father who sees in secret will Himself reward you openly. 6:2-6:3 NKJV

-It is so great to walk with Jesus!

*"Therefore, do not be like them. For your Father knows the things you have need of before you ask Him. In this manner, therefore, pray: Our Father in heaven, hallowed be your name. Your kingdom come. Your will be done on earth as it is in heaven. Give us this day our daily bread. And forgive us our debts, as we forgive our debtors. And do not lead us into temptation, but deliver us from the evil one. For yours is the kingdom and the power and the glory forever. Amen." 6:8 NKJV

-Truth that we all need to overcome darkness and should have spirits of power, love, and peace. Often, the only power you need is His abounding grace and strength in your mind.

*"But lay up for yourselves treasures in heaven, where neither moth or rust destroys and where thieves do not break in and steal." 6:20 NKJV

-This promise is great and shows how confident we should be about our home.

*"The eye is the lamp of the body. So, if your eye is healthy, your whole body will be full of light." 6:22 ESV

"The lamp of the body is the eye. If therefore your eye is good, your whole body will be full of light." 6:22 NKJV

-For me, training my eyes to be good as much as I can is a big part of what I am and my spiritual life. I try to be deep in my heart and let my eyes reflect goodness and strength. Having gentle eyes will help give you peace. Reflect the Spirit within you.

*"No one can serve two masters, for either he will hate the one and love the other, or he will be devoted to the one and despise the other. You cannot serve God and money." 6:24 ESV

"No one can serve two masters; for either he will hate the one and love the other, or else he will be loyal to the one and despise the other. You cannot serve God and mammon." 6:24 NKJV

-There is nothing in this world that is greater than the heart of the Lord!

*"But seek first the kingdom of God and his righteousness, and all these things will be added to you. Therefore, do not be anxious about tomorrow, for tomorrow will be anxious for itself. Sufficient for the day is its own trouble." 6:33 ESV

"But seek first the kingdom of God and His righteousness, and all these things shall be added to you. Therefore, do not worry about tomorrow, for tomorrow will worry about its own things. Sufficient for the day is its own trouble." 6:33 NKJV

-Awesome instruction on how to live! Day at a time, be strong in the present.

*"You hypocrite, first take the log out of your own eye, and then you will see clearly to take the speck out of your brothers' eye." 7:5 ESV

"Hypocrite! First you remove the plank from your own eye, and then you will see clearly to remove the speck from your brothers' eye." 7:5 NKJV

-You can't do anyone good without being right within yourself.

*"Ask, and it will be given to you; seek, and you will find; knock, and it will be opened to you. For everyone who asks receives, and the one who seeks finds, and to the one who knocks it will be opened." 7:7 ESV

"Ask, and it will be given to you; seek, and you will find; knock, and it will be opened to you. For everyone who asks receives, and he who seeks finds, and to him who knocks it will be opened." 7:7 NKJV

-Awesome to know that if I stay diligent and seek to accomplish great things, I can achieve it. If you are in a hard place know that if you seek to

overcome it you will. Ask the Lord for anything you may need to have a victorious life. We truly depend on Him every moment and trust Him.

*"So, whatever you wish that others would do to you, do also to them, for this is the Law and the Prophets." 7:12 ESV

"Therefore, whatever you want men to do to you, do also to them, for this is the law and the prophets." 7:12 NKJV

-Always treat others with respect and gentleness. You will find that doing this will return to you. This is very powerful because it explains how to interact with those around you and to be able to live in righteousness.

*"For the gate is narrow and the way is hard that leads to life, and those who find it are few." 7:14 ESV

"But narrow is the gate and difficult is the way that leads to life, and there are few who find it." 7:14 NKJV

*"Beware of false prophets, who come to you in sheep's clothing but inwardly are ravenous wolves. You will recognize them by their fruits. Are grapes gathered from thorn bushes, or figs from thistles? So, every healthy tree bears good fruit, but the diseased tree bears bad fruit." 7:15 ESV

"Beware of false prophets, who come to you in sheep's clothing, but inwardly they are ravenous wolves. You will know them by their fruits." 7:15 NKJV

-Important to understand that we are known by what we do. We transform. Stay true to love and justice.

*"Not everyone who says to me, 'Lord, Lord,' will enter the kingdom of heaven, but the one who does the will of my Father who is in heaven." 7:21 ESV

"Not everyone who says to Me, 'Lord, 'Lord, shall enter the kingdom of heaven, but he who does the will of my Father in heaven." 7:21 NKJV

*"And then I will declare to them, 'I never knew you; depart from Me, you who practice lawlessness!'" 7:23 NKJV

*"Everyone then who hears these words of mine and does them will be like a wise man who built his house on the rock." 7:24 ESV

"Therefore, whoever hears these sayings of Mine, and does them, I will liken to be a wise man who built his house on the rock." 7:24 NKJV

*"Those who are well have no need of a physician, but those who are sick. Go and learn what this means, I desire mercy, and not sacrifice. For I came not to call the righteous, but sinners." 9:12 ESV

"And when the pharisees saw it, they said to His disciples, 'Why does your teacher eat with tax collectors and sinners?' When Jesus heard that, He said to them, "Those who are well have no need of a physician, but those who are sick. But go and learn what this means: 'I desire mercy and not sacrifice.' For I did not come to call the righteous, but sinners, to repentance." 9:11-9:12 NKJV

*"Then He said to His disciples, "The harvest is plentiful, but the laborers are few; therefore, pray earnestly to the Lord of the harvest to send out laborers into His harvest." 9:37 ESV

"Then He said to His disciples, "The harvest is truly plentiful, but the laborers are few. Therefore, pray the Lord of the harvest to send out laborers into His harvest." 9:37 NKJV

*"And proclaim as you go, saying, "The kingdom of heaven is at hand. Heal the sick, raise the dead, cleanse lepers, cast out demons. You received without paying; give without pay." 10:7 ESV

"And as you go, preach, saying, 'The kingdom of heaven is at hand.' Heal the sick, cleanse the lepers, raise the dead, cast out demons. Freely you have received, freely give." 10:7 NKJV

*"Behold, I am sending you out as sheep in the midst of wolves, so be wise as serpents and innocent as doves." 10:16 ESV

"Behold, I send you out as sheep in the midst of wolves. Therefore, be as wise as serpents and harmless as doves." 10:16 NKJV

-This verse has been a great inspiration and fortress. For me to be wise as serpents means to be patient and understand God's word and conduct myself in Christ. Hold on to purity and principles of righteousness. The power of Jesus wins the battle we walk thru it.

*"and you will be hated by all for my name's sake. But the one who endures to the end will be saved." 10:22 ESV

"And you will be hated by all for My name's sake. But he who endures to the end will be saved." 10:22 NKJV

-You may be hated but respond in peace and love. Jesus set the example and we follow until the end as He did.

*"So, everyone who acknowledges me before men, I also will acknowledge before my Father who is in heaven." 10:32 ESV

"Therefore, whoever confesses Me before men, he I will also confess before My Father who is in heaven. But whoever denies Me before men, him I will also deny before My Father who is in heaven." 10:32 NKJV

*"... I have not come to bring peace, but a sword." 10:34 ESV

"Do not think that I came to bring peace on earth. I did not come to bring peace but a sword." 10:34 NKJV

-This sword is a rock and light in this fallen dark world. Hope!

*"And whoever does not take his cross and follow me is not worthy of me." 10:38 ESV

"And he who does not take his cross and follow after Me is not worthy of Me." 10:38 NKJV

-We serve an awesome King.

*"Take my yoke upon you, and learn from me, for I am gentle and lowly in heart, and you will find rest for your souls. For my yoke is easy, and my burden is light." 11:29 ESV

"Take My yoke upon you and learn from Me, for I am gentle and lowly in heart, and you will find rest for your souls. For My yoke is easy and My burden is light." 11:29 NKJV

*"until He brings justice to victory; and in His name the gentiles will hope." 12:20 ESV

-When I am facing adversity, I am reminded of this, in His name I will hope.

*"Knowing their thoughts, he said to them, "Every kingdom divided against itself is laid waste, and no city or house divided against itself will stand." 12:25 ESV

"But Jesus knew their thoughts, and said to them: 'Every kingdom divided against itself is brought to desolation, and every city or house divided against itself will not stand." 12:25 NKJV

- Let us be united!

*"for by your words you will be justified, and by your words you will be condemned." 12:37 ESV

"For by your words you will be justified, and by your words you will be condemned." 12:37 NKJV

-Always practice self-control.

*"As for what was sown on good soil, this is the one who hears the word and understands it. He indeed bears fruit and yields, in one case a hundredfold, in another sixty, and another thirty." 13:23 ESV

"But he who received seed on the good ground is he who hears the word and understands it, who indeed bears fruit and produces: some a hundredfold, some sixty, some thirty." 13:23 NKJV

-Understanding the gospel is very important and know that the truth sets us free! Be meek but strong, alert and peaceful. Be a light and think positive always. Trust in Jesus and the words of life.

*"He put another parable before them, saying, "The kingdom of heaven is like a grain of mustard seed that a man took and sowed in his field. It is the smallest of all seeds, but when it has grown it is larger than all the garden plants and becomes a tree, so that the birds of the air come and make nests in its branches." 13:31 ESV

"Another parable He put forth to them, saying: "The kingdom of heaven is like a mustard seed, which a man took and sowed in his field, which indeed is the least of all the seeds; but when it is grown it is greater than the herbs and becomes a tree, so that the birds of the air come and nest in its branches." 13:31 NKJV

-Truth about the church.

*"He answered, "the one who sows the good seed is the Son of Man. The field is the world, and the good seed is the sons of the kingdom." 13:37 ESV

"He answered and said to them: "He who sows the good seed is the Son of Man. The field is the world, the good seeds are the sons of the kingdom, but the tares are the sons of the wicked one." 13:37 NKJV

*"The Son of Man will send out His angels, and they will gather out of His kingdom all things that offend, and those who practice lawlessness, and will cast them into the furnace of fire." 13:41 NKJV

*"But immediately Jesus spoke to them, saying, "Take heart; it is I. Do not be afraid." 14:27 ESV

"But immediately Jesus spoke to them, saying, "Be of good cheer! It is I; do not be afraid." 14:27 NKJV

-And He is always there! Life is hard but we can have confidence in Him. What we do is through these hard times, trials, and suffering is learn from what we experience. Our skin becomes thicker and we build character and humility. The power of prayer is always necessary and don't give up. You will become a conqueror.

*"Jesus immediately reached out his hand and took hold of him, saying to him, O you of little faith, why did you doubt?" 14:31 ESV

"And immediately Jesus stretched out His hand and caught him, and said to him, "O you of little faith, why did you doubt?" 14:31 NKJV

-Faith comes in when you face something you have no other way. You can always face things and be weak but still strong at the same time.

*"And I also say to you that you are Peter, and on this rock, I will build My church, and the gates of Hades shall not prevail against it. And I will give you the keys of the kingdom of heaven, and whatever you bind on earth will be bound in heaven, and whatever you loose on earth will be loosed in heaven." 16:18 NKJV

*"For the Son of Man has come to save that which was lost." 18:11 NKJV

*"Moreover, if your brother sins against you, go and tell him his fault between you and him alone." 18:15 NKJV

*"For where two or three are gathered together in My name, I am there in the midst of them." 18:20 NKJV

-Often when I am in a bad place, I need to be with someone and pray together because this is very true. There is strength when we are together.

*"But Jesus looked at them and said, "With man this is impossible, but with God all things are possible." 19:26 ESV

"But Jesus looked at them and said to them, "With men this is impossible, but with God all things are possible." 19:26 NKJV

*"It shall not be so among you. But whoever would be great among you must be your servant, and whoever would be first among you must be your slave, even as the Son of Man came not to be served but to serve, and to give his life as a ransom for many." 20:26 ESV

"Yet it shall not be so among you, but whoever desires to become great among you, let him be your servant. And whoever desires to be first among you, let him be your slave- just as the Son of Man did not come to be served, but to serve, and to give His life a ransom for many." 20:26 NKJV

-Amazing to know that God Himself was a servant to save all people.

*"And He said to them, "It is written, my house shall be called a house of prayer, 'but you have made it a den of thieves." 21:13 NKJV

-Love righteousness and that which is good.

*"You shall love the Lord your God with all your heart and with all your soul and with all your mind. This is the great and first commandment. And the second is like it: you shall love your neighbor as yourself. On these two commandments depend all the Law and the Prophets." 22:37 ESV

"Jesus said to him, 'You shall love the Lord your God with all your heart, with all your soul, and with all your mind.' This is the first and great commandment. And the second is like it: 'You shall love your neighbor as yourself.' On these two commandments hang all the law and the prophets." 22:37 NKJV

-*There is complete freedom in Christ! REJOICE!!! When Jesus is enthroned on your heart you can overcome anything.*

Mark

*"The sower sows the word." 4:14 ESV

"The sower sows the word." 4:14 NKJV

-*Understanding the word is your armor.*

*"But those that were sown on the good soil are the ones who hear the word and accept it and bear fruit, thirtyfold and sixtyfold and a hundredfold." 4:20 ESV

"But these are the ones sown on good ground, those who hear the word, accept it, and bear fruit." 4:20 NKJV

*"And he said, "With what can we compare the kingdom of God, or what parable shall we use for it? It is like a grain of mustard seed, which, when sowed on the ground, is the smallest of all the seeds on earth, yet when it is sown it grows up and becomes larger than all the garden plants and puts out large branches, so that the birds of the air can make nests in its shade." 4:30 ESV

"Then He said, "To what shall we liken the kingdom of God? Or with what parable shall we picture it? It is like a mustard seed which, when it is sown on the ground, is smaller than all the seeds on the earth; but when it is sown, it grows up and becomes greater than all herbs, and shoots out large branches, so that the birds of the air may nest under its shade." 4:30 NKJV

-*Again, we see the church on the earth.*

*"And on the sabbath he began to teach in the synagogue, and many who heard him were astonished, saying," Where did this man get these things? What is the wisdom given to him? How are such mighty works done by his hands?" 6:2 ESV

"And when the Sabbath had come, He began to teach in the synagogue. And many hearing Him were astonished, saying, "Where did this Man get these things? And what wisdom is this which is given to Him, that such mighty works are performed by His hands? 6:2 NKJV

-This helps my understanding of how awesome Jesus is.

*"Whoever desires to come after Me, let him deny himself, and take up his cross, and follow Me." 8:34 NKJV

-Nothing compares with that freedom.

*"Jesus said to him, "If you can believe, all things are possible to him who believes. "Immediately the father of the child cried out and said with tears, "Lord, I believe, help my unbelief!" 9:23 NKJV

-I think we all have doubts from time to time. Often it is our minds trying to understand that which is true. It is important to tell Jesus what is on your heart and ask Him for whatever you need. By doing this you make it possible to grow deeper in your faith. Abide in Him! It is a lifelong process to achieve what you are made for.

*"Whoever receives one of these little children in My name receives Me; and whoever receives Me, receives not Me but Him who sent Me." 9:37 NKJV

*"But Jesus said, "Do not stop him, for no one who does a mighty work in my name will be able soon afterward to speak evil of me. For the one who is not against us is for us." 9:39 ESV

"But Jesus said, "Do not forbid him, for no one who works a miracle in My name can soon afterward speak evil of Me. For he who is not against us is on our side." 9:39 NKJV

-I always think this is cool because it says that those who are not against us are on our side!

*"Salt is good, but if the salt loses its flavor, how will you season it? Have salt in yourselves, and have peace with one another." 9:50 NKJV

-This is beautiful and portrays how our spirits are to be mighty in peace and love. Don't lose the peace and strength in your heart. If you are losing these things Jesus wants us to turn and receive Him.

*"Truly, I say to you, whoever does not receive the kingdom of God like a child shall not enter it." 10:15 ESV

"Assuredly, I say to you, whoever does not receive the kingdom of God as a little child will by no means enter it." 10:15 NKJV

-We are men and women but still children in our hearts.

*"Have you not read the scripture: "The stone that the builders rejected has become the cornerstone; this was the Lord's doing, and it is marvelous in our eyes." 12:10 ESV

"Have you not even read this scripture: The stone which the builders rejected has become the chief cornerstone. This was the Lord's doing, and it is marvelous in our eyes." 12:10 NKJV

*"Jesus answered, "The most important is, Hear O Israel: The Lord our God, the Lord is one. And you shall love the Lord your God with all your heart and with all your soul and with all your mind and with all your strength. The second is this: You shall love your neighbor as yourself. There is no other commandment greater than these." 12:29 ESV

"Jesus answered him, "The first of all the commandments is: Hear, O Israel, the Lord our God, the Lord is one. And you shall love the Lord your God with all your heart, with all your soul, with all your mind, and with all your strength.' This is the first commandment. And the second, like it, is this: 'You shall love your neighbor as yourself.' There is no other commandment greater than these." So, the scribe said to Him, "Well said, Teacher. You have spoken the truth, for there is one God, and there is no other but He. And to love Him with all the heart, with all the understanding, with all the soul, and with all the strength, and to love one's neighbor as oneself, is more than all the whole burnt offerings and sacrifices." Now when Jesus saw that he answered wisely, He said to him, "You are not far from the kingdom of God." 12:29-12:34 NKJV

-To do this is life at its fullest.

*"And when you hear of wars and rumors of wars, do not be alarmed. This must take place, but the end is not yet." 13:7 ESV

"But when you hear of wars and rumors of wars, do not be troubled; for such things must happen, but the end is not yet. 13:7 NKJV

*"And you will be hated by all for my name's sake. But the one who endures to the end will be saved." 13:13 ESV

"And you will be hated by all for My name's sake. But he who endures to the end will be saved." 13:13 NKJV

-Important to know you will not quit. Things are always darkest before there is a breakthrough. Tribulation creates you, you just need to be still and trust in peace no matter what adversity you are facing.

*"And what I say to you I say to all: Stay awake." 13:37 ESV

"And what I say to you, I say to all: Watch!" 13:37 NKJV

-Use your mind as best you can and be alert and strong. It is normal to endure all kinds of adversity. Be diligent in guarding your heart and mind. Guard your thoughts and fortify yourself. If you are under attack fix your eyes and let your Spirit of power have authority.

*"Watch and pray that you may not enter into temptation. The spirit indeed is willing, but the flesh is weak." 14:38 ESV

"Watch and pray, lest you enter into temptation. The spirit indeed is willing, but the flesh is weak." 14:38 NKJV

Luke

*"He will also go before Him in the spirit and the power of Elijah, 'to turn the hearts of the fathers to the children,' and the disobedient to the wisdom of the just, to make ready a people prepared for the Lord." 1:17 NKJV

-Discipline yourselves in your conduct and understanding. Jesus transforms hearts.

*"He has shown strength with His arm; He has scattered the proud in the thoughts of their hearts; He has brought down the mighty from their thrones and exalted those of humble estate." 1:51 ESV

"He has shown strength with His arm; He has scattered the proud in the imagination of their hearts. He has put down the mighty from their thrones, and exalted the lowly." 1:51 NKJV

*"that we, being delivered from the hand of our enemies, might serve Him without fear, in holiness and righteousness before Him all our days." 1:74

"To grant us that we, being delivered from the hand of our enemies, might serve Him without fear, in holiness and righteousness before Him all the days of our life." 1:74 NKJV

-Awesome purpose!

*"To give knowledge of salvation to His people in the forgiveness of their sins, because of the tender mercy of our God, whereby the sunrise shall visit us from on high to give light to those who sit in darkness and in the shadow of death, to guide our feet into the way of peace." 1:77 ESV

"To give knowledge of salvation to His people by the remission of their sins, through the tender mercy of our God, with which the Dayspring from on high has visited us; to give light to those who sit in darkness and the shadow of death, to guide our feet into the way of peace." 1:77 NKJV

-For me this is what life and salvation is all about.

*"And behold, an angel of the Lord stood before them, and the glory of the Lord shone around them, and they were greatly afraid. Then the angel said to them, "Do not be afraid, for behold, I bring you good tidings of great joy which will be to all people. For there is born to you this day in the city of David a Savior, who is Christ the Lord." 2:9 NKJV

*"Glory to God in the highest, and on earth peace, goodwill toward men!" 2:14 NKJV

*"Bear fruits in keeping with repentance." 3:8 ESV

"Therefore, bear fruits worthy of repentance." 3:8 NKJV

*"Whoever has two tunics is to share with him who has none, and whoever has food is to do likewise." 3:11 ESV

"He answered and said to them, "He who has two tunics, let him give to him who has none; and he who has food, let him do likewise." 3:11 NKJV

*"The Spirit of the Lord is upon me, because He has anointed Me to proclaim good news to the poor. He has sent Me to proclaim liberty to the captives and recovering of sight to the blind, to set at liberty those who are oppressed, to proclaim the year of the Lord's favor." 4:18 ESV

"The Spirit of the Lord is upon Me, because He has anointed Me to preach the gospel to the poor; He has sent Me to heal the brokenhearted, to proclaim liberty to the captives and recovery of sight to the blind, to set at liberty those who are oppressed; to proclaim the acceptable year of the Lord." 4:18 NKJV

-YEAAAAAAA!!! Bold in the power of the Lord and His love.

*"Jesus answered and said to them, those who are well have no need of a physician, but those who are sick. I have not come to call the righteous, but sinners, to repentance." 5:31 NKJV

*"For no good tree bears bad fruit, nor again does a bad tree bear good fruit, for each tree is known by its own fruit." 6:43 ESV

"For a good tree does not bear bad fruit, nor does a bad tree bear good fruit. For every tree is known by its own fruit." 6:43 NKJV

*"But why do you call Me 'Lord, Lord,' and not do the things which I say? Whoever comes to Me, and hears my sayings and does them, I will show you whom he is like he is like a man building a house, who dug deep and laid the foundation on the rock. And when the flood arose, the stream beat vehemently against that house, and could not shake it, for it was founded on the rock." 6:46 NKJV

*"As for that in the good soil, they are those who, hearing the word, hold it fast in an honest and good heart, and bear fruit with patience." 8:15 ESV

"But the ones that fell on the good ground are those who, having heard the word with a noble and good heart, keep it and bear fruit with patience." 8:15 NKJV

-*Powerful!*

*"But He answered them, "My mother and my brothers are those who hear the word of God and do it." 8:21 ESV

"But He answered and said to them, My mother and My brothers are these who hear the word of God and do it." 8:21 NKJV

*"And He said to her, "Daughter, be of good cheer; your faith has made you well. Go in peace." 8:48 NKJV

-*Grace!!*

*"But Jesus said to him, "Do not stop him, for the one who is not against you is for you." 9:50 ESV

"But Jesus said to him, "Do not forbid him, for he who is not against us is on our side." 9:50 NKJV

*"But He turned and rebuked them, and said, "You do not know what manner of spirit you are of. For the Son of Man did not come to destroy men's lives but to save them." 9:55 NKJV

*"But Jesus said to him, "No one, having put his hand to the plow, and looking back, is fit for the kingdom of God." 9:62 NKJV

*"And He said to them, "The harvest is plentiful, but the laborers are few. Therefore, pray earnestly to the Lord of the harvest to send out laborers into His harvest. Go your way; behold, I am sending you out as lambs in the midst of wolves." 10:2 ESV

"Then He said to them, "the harvest truly is great, but the laborers are few; therefore, pray the Lord of the harvest to send out laborers into His harvest. Go your way; behold, I send you out as lambs among wolves." 10:2 NKJV

-This is very true the enemy is there and we need Jesus to stand. Practice these things and don't fear. If you are afraid understand that fear can drive faith too. Fear is a reaction, courage is decision.

*"Behold, I have given you authority to tread on serpents and scorpions, and over all the power of the enemy, and nothing shall hurt you. Nevertheless, do not rejoice in this, that the spirits are subject to you, but rejoice that your names are written in heaven." 10:19 ESV

"Behold, I give you the authority to trample on serpents and scorpions, and over all the power of the enemy, and nothing shall by any means hurt you." 10:19 NKJV

***"He said to him, "What is written in the law? What is your reading of it?" So, he answered and said, "You shall love the Lord your God with all your heart, with all your soul, and with all your strength, and with all your mind, and love your neighbor as yourself." And He said to him," You have answered rightly; do this and you will live." 10:26 NKJV

*"And he said, "He who showed mercy on him." Then Jesus said to him, "Go and do likewise." 10:37 NKJV

***"And I tell you, ask, and it will be given to you; seek, and you will find; knock, and it will be opened to you. For everyone who asks receives, and the one who seeks finds, and to the one who knocks it will be opened." 11:9 ESV

"So, I say to you, ask, and it will be given to you; seek, and you will find; knock, and it will be opened to you. For everyone who asks receives, and he who seeks finds, and to him who knocks it will be opened." 11:9 NKJV

-I love this because you know that seeking Him and His righteousness is always possible, and you can receive anything God would want for you. These things can take time. Be patient and wait on the Lord.

*"But He, knowing their thoughts, said to them, "Every kingdom divided against itself is laid waste, and a divided household falls." 11:17 ESV

He, knowing their thoughts, said to them: "Every kingdom divided against itself is brought to desolation, and a house divided against a house falls." 11:17 NKJV

*"Likewise, I say to you, there is joy in the presence of the angels of God over one sinner who repents." 15:10 NKJV

***"nor will they say, 'See here!' or 'See there!' For indeed, the kingdom of God is within you." 17:21 NKJV

-Be diligent in doing this.

***"Then He spoke a parable to them, that men always ought to pray and not lose heart." 18:1 NKJV

-The world will come against you. But when you stay consistent and keep fighting back in faith and peace you will succeed. I am reminded of this scripture every day.

***"Truly I say to you, whoever does not receive the kingdom of God like a child shall not enter it," 18:17 ESV

"Assuredly, I say to you, whoever does not receive the kingdom of God as a little child will by no means enter it." 18:17 NKJV

*"Now He is not God of the dead, but of the living, for all live to Him." 20:38 ESV

"For He is not the God of the dead but of the living, for all live to Him." 20:38 NKJV

-King of Glory

John

***"In Him was life, and the life was the light of men. The light shines in the darkness, and the darkness has not overcome it." 1:4 ESV

"In Him was life, and the life was the light of men. And the light shines in the darkness, and the darkness did not comprehend it." 1:4 NKJV

*"The true light, which gives light to everyone, was coming into the world." 1:9 ESV

"That was the true light which gives light to every man coming into the world. He was in the world, and the world was made through Him, and the world did not know Him." 1:9 NKJV

-He is truly amazing!

*"But to all who did receive Him, who believed in His name, He gave the right to become children of God, who were born, not of blood nor of the will of the flesh nor of the will of man, but of God." 1:12 ESV

"But as many as received Him, to them He gave the right to become children of God, to those who believe in His name: who were born, not of blood, nor of the will of the flesh, nor of the will of man, but of God." 1:12 NKJV

*"Jesus answered him, "Truly, truly, I say to you, unless one is born again, he cannot see the kingdom of God." 3:3 ESV

"Jesus answered and said to him, "Most assuredly, I say to you, unless one is born again, he cannot see the kingdom of God." 3:3 NKJV

*"For God did not send His Son into the world to condemn the world, but in order that the world might be saved through Him... And this is the judgment: the light has come into the world, and people loved the darkness rather than the light because their works were evil." 3:17 ESV

"For God did not send His Son into the world to condemn the world, but that the world through Him might be saved... And this is the condemnation, that the light has come into the world, and men loved darkness rather than light, because their deeds were evil." 3:17 NKJV

*"But whoever does what is true comes to the light, so that it may be clearly seen that his works have been carried out in God." 3:21 ESV

"But he who does the truth comes to the light, that his deeds may be clearly seen, that they have been done in God." 3:21 NKJV

-Very powerful promise!

*"Whoever believes in the Son has eternal life; whoever does not obey the Son shall not see life, but the wrath of God remains on him." 3:36 ESV

*"For in this the saying is true: 'One sows and another reaps. I sent you to reap that for which you have not labored; others have labored, and you have entered into their labors." 4:37 NKJV

-Very true. Respect!

*"Do not work for the food that perishes, but for the food that endures to eternal life, which the Son of Man will give to you. For on him God the Father has set His seal." 6:27 ESV

*"Jesus answered them, "This is the work of God, that you believe in Him whom He has sent." 6:29 ESV

"Jesus answered and said to them, "This is the work of God, that you believe in Him whom He sent." 6:29 NKJV

*"For the bread of God is He who comes down from heaven and gives life to the world." 6:33 ESV

*"All that the Father gives Me will come to Me, and whoever comes to Me I will never cast out." 6:37 ESV

-Knowing this, don't give up or worry!

*"It is written in the Prophets, 'And they all will be taught by God.' Everyone who has heard and learned from the Father comes to Me-" 6:45 ESV

*"It is the Spirit who gives life; the flesh is no help at all. The words that I have spoken to you are spirit and life." 6:63 ESV

*"The one who speaks on his own authority seeks his own glory; but the one who seeks the glory of Him who sent Him is true, and in him there is no falsehood." 7:18 ESV

"He who speaks from himself seeks his own glory; but He who seeks the glory of the One who sent Him is true, and no unrighteousness is in Him." 7:18 NKJV

-A wonderful purpose!

*"On the last day of the feast, the great day, Jesus stood up and cried out, "If anyone thirsts, let him come to Me and drink. Whoever believes in Me, as the scripture has said, 'Out of his heart will flow rivers of living water.'" 7:37 ESV

-Truth is our peace and comfort.

*"Again, Jesus spoke to them, saying, "I am the light of the world. Whoever follows Me will not walk in darkness, but will have the light of life." 8:12 ESV

"Then Jesus spoke to them again, saying, "I am the light of the world. He who follows Me shall not walk in darkness, but have the light of life." 8:12 NKJV

*"If you abide in My word, you are truly my disciples, and you will know the truth, and the truth will set you free." 8:31 ESV

"If you abide in My word, you are My disciples indeed. And you shall know the truth, and the truth shall make you free." 8:31 NKJV

*"Jesus answered them, "Truly, truly, I say to you, everyone who practices sin is a slave to sin." 8:34 ESV

*"Jesus said to them, "If God were your Father, you would love me, for I came from God and I am here. I came not of my own accord, but He sent Me." 8:42 ESV

*"Truly, truly, I say to you, if anyone keeps my word, he will never see death." 8:51 ESV

"Most assuredly, I say to you, if anyone keeps My word, he shall never see death." 8:51 NKJV

*"I am the door. If anyone enters by Me, he will be saved and will go in and out and find pasture. The thief comes only to steal and kill and destroy. I came that they may have life and have it abundantly." 10:9 ESV

"I am the door. If anyone enters by Me, he will be saved, and will go in and out and find pasture. The thief does not come except to steal, and to kill, and to destroy. I have come that they may have life, and that they may have it more abundantly." 10:9 NKJV

***"I have come into the world as light, so that whoever believes in Me may not remain in darkness. If anyone hears My words and does not keep them, I do not judge him; for I did not come to judge the world but to save the world." 12:46 ESV

"I have come as a light into the world, that whoever believes in Me should not abide in darkness. And if anyone hears My words and does not believe, I do not judge him; for I did not come to judge the world but to save the world." 12:46 NKJV

***"You call Me Teacher and Lord, and you are right, for so I am. If I then, your Lord and Teacher, have washed your feet, you also ought to wash one another's feet. For I have given you an example, that you also should do just as I have done to you." 13:13 ESV

"You call Me Teacher and Lord, and you say well, for so I am. If I then, your Lord and Teacher, have washed your feet, you also ought to wash one another's feet. For I have given you and example, that you should do as I have done to you." 13:13 NKJV

-WWJD (what would Jesus do) He truly set the perfect example for us and in difficult times just remember to do what He would do.

*"Truly, truly, I say to you, whoever receives the one I send receives Me, and whoever receives Me receives the one who sent Me." 13:20 ESV

"Most assuredly, I say to you, he who receives whomever I send receives Me; and he who receives Me receives Him who sent Me." 13:20 NKJV

***"A new commandment I give to you, that you love one another: just as I have loved you, you also are to love one another. By this all people will know that you are My disciples, if you have love for one another." 13:34 ESV

"A new commandment I give to you, that you love one another; as I have loved you, that you also love one another. By this all will know that you are My disciples, if you have love for one another." 13:34 NKJV

*"Let not your hearts be troubled. Believe in God; believe also in Me." 14:1 ESV

"Let not your heart be troubled; you believe in God, believe also in Me." 14:1 NKJV

*"Jesus said to him, "I am the way, and the truth, and the life. No one comes to the Father except through Me. If you had known Me, you would have known My Father also. From now on you do know Him and have seen Him." 14:6 ESV

"Jesus said to him, "I am the way, the truth, and the life. No one comes to the Father except through Me. If you had known Me, you would have known My Father also; and from now on you know Him and have seen Him." 14:6 NKJV

*"Jesus said to him, "Have I been with you so long, and you still do not know Me, Phillip? Whoever has seen Me has seen the Father. How can you say, show us the Father? Do you not believe that I am in the Father and the Father is in Me? The words that I say to you I do not speak on My own authority, but the Father who dwells in Me does His works. Believe Me that I am in the Father and the Father is in Me, or else believe on account of the works themselves." 14:9 ESV

"Jesus said to him, "Have I been with you so long, and yet you have not known Me, Phillip? He who has seen Me has seen the Father; so how can you say, 'Show us the Father?' Do you not believe that I am in the Father, and the Father in Me? The words that I speak to you I do not speak on My own authority; but the Father who dwells in Me does the works. Believe Me that I am in the Father and the Father in Me, or else believe Me for the sake of the works themselves." 14:9 NKJV

***"Every branch in Me that does not bear fruit He takes away, and every branch that does bear fruit He prunes, that it may bear more fruit. Already you are clean because of the word that I have spoken to you. Abide in Me, and I in you. As the branch cannot bear fruit by itself, unless it abides in the vine, neither can you, unless you abide in Me." 15:2 ESV

"Every branch in Me that does not bear fruit He takes away; and every branch that bears fruit He prunes, that it may bear more fruit. You are already clean because of the word which I have spoken to you. Abide in Me, and I in you. As the branch cannot bear fruit of itself, unless it abides in the vine, neither can you, unless you abide in Me." 15:2 NKJV

-Truly awesome to be given this.

*"By this My Father is glorified, that you bear much fruit and so prove to be my disciples. As the Father has loved Me, so have I loved you. Abide in My love. If you keep My commandments, you will abide in My love, just as I have kept My Father's commandments and abide in His love. These things I have spoken to you, that My joy may be in you, and that your joy may be full." 15:8 ESV

"By this My Father is glorified, that you bear much fruit; so, you will be My disciples. As the Father loved Me, I also have loved you; abide in My love. If you keep My commandments, you will abide in My love, just as I have kept My Father's commandments and abide in His love. These things I have spoken to you, that My joy may remain in you, and that your joy may be full." 15:8 NKJV

*"If the world hates you, know that it has hated Me before it hated you. If you were of the world, the world would love you as its own; but because you are not of the world, but I chose you out of the world, therefore the world hates you." 15:18 ESV

"If the world hates you, you know that it hated Me before it hated you. If you were of the world, the world would love its own. Yet because you are not of the world, but I chose you out of the world, therefore the world hates you." 15:18 NKJV

*"They will put you out of the synagogues. Indeed, the hour is coming when whoever kills you will think he is offering service to God. And they will do these things because they have not known the Father, nor Me." 16:2 ESV

"They will put you out of the synagogues; yes, the time is coming that whoever kills you will think that he offers God service. And these things they will do to you because they have not known the Father nor Me. But these things I have told you, that when the time comes, you may remember that I told you them." 16:2 NKJV

*"Truly, truly, I say to you, you will weep and lament, but the world will rejoice. You will be sorrowful, but your sorrow will turn into joy." 16:20 ESV

"Most assuredly, I say to you that you will weep and lament, but the world will rejoice; and you will be sorrowful, but your sorrow will be turned into joy." 16:20 NKJV

*"Until now you have asked nothing in My name. Ask, and you will receive, that your joy may be full." 16:24 ESV

"Until now you have asked nothing in My name. Ask, and you will receive, that your joy may be full." 16:24 NKJV

***"I have said these things to you, that in Me you may have peace. In the world you will have tribulation. But take heart; I have overcome the world." 16:33 ESV

"These things I have spoken to you, that in Me you may have peace. In the world you will have tribulation; but be of good cheer, I have overcome the world." 16:33 NKJV

*"And this is eternal life, that they know you the only true God, and Jesus Christ whom you have sent. I glorified you on earth, having accomplished the work that you gave Me to do." 17:3 ESV

"And this is eternal life, that they may know You, the only true God, and Jesus Christ whom You have sent. I have glorified You on the earth. I have finished the work which You have given Me to do." 17:3 NKJV

*"And I am no longer in the world, but they are in the world, and I am coming to you. Holy Father, keep them in Your name, which You have given Me, that they may be as one, even as we are one." 17:11 ESV

*"I have given them Your word, and the world has hated them because they are not of the world, just as I am not of the world. I do not ask that You take them out of the world, but that you keep them from the evil one." 17:14 ESV

***"As You sent Me into the world, so I have sent them into the world." 17:18 ESV

*"And the glory which You gave Me I have given them, that they may be one just as We are one." 17:22 NKJV

*"Jesus answered, "You say rightly that I am a king. For this cause I was born, and for this cause I have come into the world, that I should

bear witness to the truth. Everyone who is of the truth hears My voice." 18:37 NKJV

*"but these are written that you may believe that Jesus is the Christ, the Son of God, and that believing you may have life in His name." 20:31 NKJV

Acts

*"And it shall come to pass that everyone who calls on the name of the Lord shall be saved." 2:21 ESV

"And it shall come to pass that whoever calls on the name of the Lord shall be saved." 2:21 NKJV

***"For David says concerning Him, "I saw the Lord always before me, for He is at my right hand that I may not be shaken; therefore my heart was glad, and my tongue rejoiced; my flesh also will dwell in hope. For You will not abandon my soul to Hades or let your holy one sees corruption. You have made known to me the paths of life; you will make me full of gladness with Your presence." 2:25 ESV

-This is so great and such a great promise!

*"And Peter said to them, "Repent and be baptized every one of you in the name of Jesus Christ for the forgiveness of your sins, and you will receive the gift of the Holy Spirit. For the promise is for you and for your children and for all who are far off, everyone whom the Lord our God calls to Himself." And with many other words he bore witness and continued to exhort them, saying, "Save yourselves from this crooked generation." 2:38 ESV

"Then Peter said to them, "Repent, and let every one of you be baptized in the name of Jesus Christ for the remission of sins; and you shall receive the gift of the Holy Spirit. For the promise is to you and to your children, and to all who are afar off, as many as the Lord our God will call." And with many other words he testified and exhorted them, saying, "Be saved from this perverse generation." 2:38 NKJV

-Yes, it is true the world is a harsh place. But to know that in us is a Spirit of promise is a rock for my faith.

*"This Jesus is the stone that was rejected by you, the builders, which has become the cornerstone. And there is salvation in no one else, for there

is no other name under heaven given among men by which we must be saved." 4:11 ESV

"This is the stone which was rejected by you builders, which has become the chief cornerstone. Nor is there salvation in any other, for there is no other name under heaven given among men by which we must be saved." 4:11 NKJV

*"But Peter and the apostles answered, "We must obey God rather than men. The God of our fathers raised Jesus, whom you killed by hanging Him on a tree. God exalted Him at His right hand as Leader and Savior, to give repentance to Israel and forgiveness of sins. And we are witnesses to these things, and so is the Holy Spirit, whom God has given to those who obey Him." 5:29 ESV

*"Heaven is My throne, and earth is My footstool. What house will you build for Me? Says the Lord, or what is the place of My rest? Has My hand not made all these things?" 7:49 NKJV

*"Then the churches throughout all Judea, Galilee, and Samaria had peace and were edified. And walking in the fear of the Lord and in the comfort of the Holy Spirit, they were multiplied." 9:31 NKJV

*"So, Peter opened his mouth and said: "Truly I understand that God shows no partiality, but in any nation anyone who fears Him and does what is right is acceptable to Him." 10:34 ESV

"But in every nation whoever fears Him and works righteousness is accepted by Him. The word which God sent to the children of Israel, preaching peace through Jesus Christ- He is Lord of all-" 10:35 NKJV

-Awesome!!!

*"For so the Lord has commanded us, saying, "I have made you a light for the gentiles, that you may bring salvation to the ends of the earth." 13:47 ESV

"For so the Lord has commanded us: I have set you as a light to the gentiles, that you should be for salvation to the ends of the earth." 13:47 NKJV

***"strengthening the souls of the disciples, encouraging them to continue in the faith, and saying that through many tribulations we must enter the kingdom of God." 14:22 ESV

"strengthening the souls of the disciples, exhorting them to continue in the faith, and saying, "We must through many tribulations enter the kingdom of God." 14:22 NKJV

-Take heart! You are not alone!

*"Believe in the Lord Jesus, and you will be saved, you and your household." 16:31 ESV

*"So, they said, "Believe on the Lord Jesus Christ, and you will be saved, you and your household." 16:31 NKJV

*"In all things I have shown you that by working hard in this way we must help the weak and remember the words of the Lord Jesus, how He Himself said, 'It is more blessed to give than to receive." 20:35 ESV

"I have shown you in every way, by laboring like this, that you must support the weak. And remember the words of the Lord Jesus, that He said, 'It is more blessed to give than to receive." 20:35 NKJV

*"delivering you from your people and from the gentiles- to whom I am sending you to open their eyes, so that they may turn from darkness to light and from the power of Satan to God, that they may receive forgiveness of sins and a place among those who are sanctified by faith in Me." 26:17 ESV

"I will deliver you from the Jewish people, as well as from the gentiles, to whom I now send you, to open their eyes, in order to turn them from darkness to light, and from the power of Satan to God, that they may receive forgiveness of sins and an inheritance among those who are sanctified by faith in Me." 26:17 NKJV

-Jesus makes you stand out.

Romans

*"For God is my witness, whom I serve with my spirit in the gospel of His Son, that without ceasing I make mention of you always in my prayers." 1:9 NKJV

*"For I am not ashamed of the gospel, for it is the power of God for salvation to everyone who believes, to the Jew first and also to the Greek. For in it the righteousness of God is revealed from faith for faith, as it is written, "The righteous shall live by faith." 1:16 ESV

"For I am not ashamed of the gospel of Christ, for it is the power of God to salvation for everyone who believes, for the Jew first and also for the Greek. For in it the righteousness of God is revealed from faith to faith; as it is written, "The just shall live by faith." 1:16 NKJV

*"For the wrath of God is revealed from heaven against all ungodliness and unrighteousness of men, who by their unrighteousness suppress the truth." 1:18 ESV

"For the wrath of God is revealed from heaven against all ungodliness and unrighteousness of men, who suppress the truth in unrighteousness..." 1:18 NKJV

*"For although they knew God, they did not honor Him as God or give thanks to Him, but they became futile in their thinking, and their foolish hearts were darkened." 1:21 ESV

"because, although they knew God, they did not glorify Him as God, nor were thankful, but became futile in their thoughts, and their foolish hearts were darkened." 1:21 NKJV

*"but glory and honor and peace for everyone who does good, the Jew first and also the Greek. For God shows no partiality." 2:10 ESV

"but glory, honor, and peace to everyone who works what is good, to the Jew first and to the Greek. For there is no partiality with God." 2:10 NKJV

*"for all have sinned and fall short of the glory of God, and are justified by His grace as a gift, through the redemption that is in Christ Jesus." 3:23 ESV

"for all have sinned and fall short of the glory of God, being justified freely by His grace through the redemption that is in Christ Jesus." 3:23 NKJV

*"Blessed are those whose lawless deeds are forgiven, and whose sins are covered; blessed is the man against whom the Lord will not count his sin." 4:7 ESV

"Blessed are those whose lawless deeds are forgiven, and whose sins are covered; blessed is that man to whom the Lord shall not impute sin." 4:7 NKJV

***"Therefore, since we have been justified by faith, we have peace with God through our Lord Jesus Christ. Through Him we have also obtained access by faith into this grace in which we stand, and we rejoice in hope of the glory of God. Not only that, but we rejoice in our sufferings, knowing that suffering produces endurance, and endurance produces character, and character produces hope, and hope does not put us to shame, because God's love has been poured into our hearts through the Holy Spirit who has been given to us. For while we were still weak, at the right time Christ died for the ungodly." 5:1 ESV

"Therefore, having been justified by faith, we have peace with God through our Lord Jesus Christ, through whom also we have access by faith into this grace in which we stand, and rejoice in hope of the glory of God. And not only that, but we also glory in tribulations, knowing that tribulation produces perseverance, and perseverance, character; and character, hope. Now hope does not disappoint, because the love of God has been poured out in our hearts by the Holy Spirit who was given to us. For when we were still without strength, in due time Christ died for the ungodly." 5:1 NKJV

-THANK YOU JESUS!!!

*"but God shows His love for us in that while we were still sinners, Christ died for us. Since, therefore, we have now been justified by His blood, much more shall we be saved by Him from the wrath of God." 5:8 ESV

"But God demonstrates His own love toward us, in that while we were still sinners, Christ died for us. Much more then, having now been justified by His blood, we shall be saved from wrath through Him." 5:8 NKJV

*"so that, as sin reigned in death, grace also might reign through righteousness leading to eternal life through Jesus Christ our Lord." 5:20 ESV

"so that as sin reigned in death, even so grace might reign through righteousness to eternal life through Jesus Christ our Lord." 5:20 NKJV

*"What shall we say then? Are we to continue in sin that grace may abound? By no means! How can we who died to sin still live in it?" 6:1 ESV

"What shall we say then? Shall we continue in sin that grace may abound? Certainly not! How shall we who died to sin live any longer in it? 6:1 NKJV

***"For the death He died He died to sin, once for all, but the life He lives He lives to God. So, you also must consider yourselves dead to sin and alive to God in Christ Jesus." 6:10 ESV

"For the death that He died, He died to sin once for all; but the life that He lives, He lives to God. Likewise, you also, reckon yourselves to be dead indeed to sin, but alive to God in Christ Jesus our Lord. Therefore, do not let sin reign in your mortal body, that you should obey it in its lusts. And do not present your members as instruments of unrighteousness to sin but present yourselves to God as being alive from the dead, and your members as instruments of righteousness to God. For sin shall not have dominion over you, for you are not under law but under grace." 6:10 NKJV

*"Do you not know that if you present yourselves to anyone as obedient slaves, you are slaves of the one whom you obey, either of sin, which leads to death, or of obedience, which leads to righteousness." 6:16 ESV

*"and, having been set free from sin, have become slaves of righteousness." 6:18 ESV

"And having been set free from sin, you became slaves of righteousness." 6:18 NKJV

*"There is therefore now no condemnation for those who are in Christ Jesus. For the law of the Spirit of life has set you free in Christ Jesus from the law of sin and death." 8:1 ESV

"There is therefore now no condemnation to those who are in Christ Jesus, who do not walk according to the flesh, but according to the Spirit." 8:1 NKJV

-*Truth*

***"For to set the mind on the flesh is death, but to set the mind on the Spirit is life and peace." 8:6 ESV

-*This simple truth is so very powerful.*

*"But if Christ is in you, although the body is dead because of sin, the Spirit is life because of righteousness." 8:10 ESV

*"For if you live according to the flesh you will die, but if by the Spirit you put to death the deeds of the body, you will live." 8:13 ESV

"For if you live according to the flesh you will die; but if by the Spirit you put to death the deeds of the body, you will live." 8:13 NKJV

*"For I consider that the sufferings of this present time are not worth comparing with the glory that is to be revealed to us." 8:18 ESV

*"And we know that for those who love God all things work together for good, for those who are called according to His purpose." 8:28 ESV

"And we know that all things work together for good to those who love God, to those who are the called according to His purpose." 8:28 NKJV

*"What then shall we say to these things? If God is for us, who can be against us?" 8:31 NKJV

*"Yet in all these things we are more than conquerors through Him who loved us." 8:37 NKJV

*"For with the heart one believes unto righteousness, and with the mouth confession is made unto salvation." 10:10 NKJV

*"For there is no distinction between Jew and Greek; for the same Lord is Lord of all, bestowing His riches on all who call on Him. For everyone who calls on the name of the Lord will be saved." 10:12 ESV

"For there is no distinction between Jew and Greek, for the same Lord over all is rich to all who call upon Him. For whoever calls on the name of the Lord shall be saved." 10:12 NKJV

*"Do not be conformed to this world, but be transformed by the renewal of your mind, that by testing you may discern what is the will of God, what is good and acceptable and perfect." 12:2 ESV

-Guard your heart and mind. Your mentality and the way you control it is vital. Learn to conduct yourself in peace and power through His Spirit. You are free. Grow in your understanding and wisdom.

***"Let love be without hypocrisy. Abhor what is evil. Cling to what is good. Be kindly affectionate to one another with brotherly love, in honor giving preference to one another." 12:9 NKJV

*"If possible, so far as it depends on you, live peaceably with all." 12:18 ESV

*"May the God of hope fill you with all joy and peace in believing, so that by the power of the Holy Spirit you may abound in hope." 15:13 ESV

"Now may the God of hope fill you with all joy and peace in believing, that you may abound in hope by the power of the Holy Spirit." 15:13 NKJV

***"The God of peace will soon crush Satan under your feet. The grace of our Lord Jesus Christ be with you." 16:20 ESV

"And the god of peace will crush Satan under your feet shortly." 16:20 NKJV

-Crushers. Thank you Lord.

1 Corinthians

*"And because of him you are in Christ Jesus, who became to us wisdom from God, righteousness and sanctification and redemption, so that, as it is written, "Let the one who boasts, boast in the Lord."" 1:30 ESV

"But of Him you are in Christ Jesus, who became for us wisdom from God- and righteousness and sanctification and redemption- that, as it is written, "He who glorifies, let him glory in the Lord."" 1:30 NKJV

*"so that your faith might not rest in the wisdom of men but in the power of God." 2:5 ESV

"And my speech and my preaching were not with persuasive words of human wisdom, but in demonstration of the Spirit and of power, that your faith should not be in the wisdom of men but in the power of God." 2:4 NKJV

*"What no eye has seen, nor ear heard, nor the heart of man imagined, what God has prepared for those who love Him." 2:9 ESV

"Eye has not seen, nor ear heard, nor have entered into the heart of man the things which God has prepared for those who love Him." 2:9 NKJV

*"Now we have not received the spirit of the world, but the Spirit who is from God, that we might understand the things freely given us by God." 2:12 ESV

"Now we have received, not the spirit of the world, but the Spirit who is from God, that we might know the things that have been freely given to us by God." 2:12 NKJV

*"So, neither he who plants nor he who waters is anything, but only God who gives the growth." 3:7 ESV

"So then neither he who plants is anything, nor he who waters, but God who gives the increase." 3:7 NKJV

*"For we are God's fellow workers. You are God's field, God's building." 3:9 ESV

"For we are God's fellow workers; you are God's field, you are God's building." 3:9 NKJV

*"For no one can lay a foundation other than that which is laid, which is Jesus Christ." 3:11 ESV

*"You are already full! You are already rich! You have reigned as kings without us- and indeed I could wish you did reign, that we also might reign with you!" 4:8 NKJV

*"To the present hour we hunger and thirst, we are poorly dressed and buffeted and homeless, and we labor, working with our own hands. When reviled, we bless; when persecuted, we endure." 4:11 ESV

"And we labor, working with our own hands. Being reviled, we bless; being persecuted, we endure." 4:12 NKJV

*"Do you not know that the unrighteous will not inherit the kingdom of God?" 6:9 NKJV

*"And such were some of you. But you were washed, you were sanctified, you were justified in the name of the Lord Jesus Christ and by the Spirit of our God." 6:11 ESV

"And such were some of you. But you were washed, but you were sanctified, but you were justified in the name of the Lord Jesus and by the Spirit of our God." 6:11 NKJV

*"for you were bought with a price, so glorify God in your body." 6:20 ESV

"For you were bought at a price; therefore, glorify God in your body and in your spirit, which are God's." 6:20 NKJV

*"But I want you to be without care. He who is unmarried cares for the things of the Lord- how he may please the Lord." 7:32 NKJV

*"Even so the Lord has commanded that those who preach the gospel should live from the gospel." 9:14 NKJV

*"No temptation has overtaken you except such as is common to man; but God is faithful, who will not allow you to be tempted beyond what you are able, but with the temptation will also make the way of escape, that you may be able to bear it." 10:13 NKJV

*"Let no one seek his own good, but the good of his neighbor." 10:24 ESV

"All things are lawful for me, but not all things are helpful; all things are lawful for me, but not all things edify. Let no one seek his own, but each one the others wellbeing." 10:23 NKJV

-*The things we endure and fight for are not for ourselves but those who need us.*

*"Love suffers long and is kind; love does not envy; love does not parade itself, is not puffed up; does not behave rudely, does not seek its own, is not provoked, thinks no evil; does not rejoice in iniquity, but rejoices in the truth; bears all things, believes all things, hopes all things, endures all things." 13:4 NKJV

*"So now faith, hope, and love abide, these three; but the greatest of these is love." 13:13 ESV

*"And now abide faith, hope, love, these three; but the greatest of these is love." 13:13 NKJV

*"So, with yourselves, since you are eager for manifestations of the Spirit, strive to excel in building up the church." 14:12 ESV

"Even so you, since you are zealous for spiritual gifts, let it be for the edification of the church that you seek to excel." 14:12 NKJV

*"For God is not a God of confusion but of peace." 14:33 ESV

"For God is not the author of confusion but of peace, as in all the churches of the saints." 14:33 NKJV

*"Do not be deceived: "Bad company ruins good morals." Wake up from your drunken stupor, as is right, and do not go on sinning." 15:33 ESV

"Do not be deceived: "Evil company corrupts good habits." Awake to righteousness, and do not sin; for some do not have the knowledge of God." 15:33 NKJV

*"So is it with the resurrection of the dead. What is sown is perishable; what is raised is imperishable. It is sown in dishonor; it is raised in glory. It is sown in weakness; it is raised in power. It is sown a natural body; it is raised a spiritual body. If there is a natural body, there is also a spiritual body." 15:42 ESV

"So also, is the resurrection of the dead. The body is sown in corruption, it is raised in incorruption. It is sown in dishonor; it is raised in glory. It is sown in weakness; it is raised in power. It is sown a natural body; it is raised a spiritual body. There is a natural body, and there is a spiritual body." 15:42 NKJV

*"The sting of death is sin, and the power of sin is the law. But thanks be to God, who gives us the victory through our Lord Jesus Christ. Therefore, my beloved brothers, be steadfast, immovable, always abounding in the

work of the Lord, knowing that in the Lord your labor is not in vain." 15:56 ESV

"The sting of death is sin, and the strength of sin is the law. But thanks be to God, who gives us the victory through our Lord Jesus Christ. Therefore, my beloved brethren, be steadfast, immovable, always abounding in the work of the Lord, knowing that your labor is not in vain in the Lord." 15:56 NKJV

*"for a wide door for effective work has opened to me, and there are many adversaries." 16:9 ESV

"For a great and effective door has opened to me, and there are many adversaries." 16:9 NKJV

***"Be watchful, stand firm in the faith, act like men, be strong. Let all that you do be done in love." 16:13 ESV

"Watch, stand fast in the faith, be brave, be strong. Let all that you do be done with love." 16:13 NKJV

2 Corinthians

*"Blessed be the God and Father of our Lord Jesus Christ, the Father of mercies and God of all comfort, who comforts us in all our affliction, so that we may be able to comfort those who are in any affliction, with the comfort with which we ourselves are comforted by God. For as we share abundantly in Christ's sufferings, so through Christ we share abundantly in comfort too. If we are afflicted, it is for your comfort and salvation; and if we are comforted, it is for your comfort, which you experience when you patiently endure the same sufferings that we suffer." 1:3 ESV

"Blessed be the God and Father of our Lord Jesus Christ, the Father of mercies and God of all comfort, who comforts us in all our tribulation, that we may be able to comfort those who are in any trouble, with the comfort with which we ourselves are comforted by God. For as the sufferings of Christ abound in us, so our consolation also abounds through Christ. Now if we are afflicted, it is for your consolation and salvation, which is effective for enduring the same sufferings which we also suffer." 1:3 NKJV

***"Indeed, we felt that we had received the sentence of death. But that was to make us rely not on ourselves but on God who raises the dead." 1:9 ESV

"Yes, we had the sentence of death in ourselves, that we should not trust in ourselves but in God who raises the dead, who delivered us from so great a death, and does deliver us; in whom we trust that He will still deliver us." 1:9 NKJV

-It is not pleasant at all but He will save us.

*"so, you should rather turn to forgive and comfort him, or he may be overwhelmed by excessive sorrow. So, I beg you to reaffirm your love for him. For this is why I wrote, that I might test you and know whether you are obedient in everything." 2:7 ESV

"so that, on the contrary, you ought rather to forgive and comfort him, lest perhaps such a one be swallowed up with too much sorrow. Therefore, I urge you to reaffirm your love to him." 2:7 NKJV

-love this so much =)

*"But thanks be to God, who in Christ always leads us in triumphal procession, and through us spreads the fragrance of the knowledge of Him everywhere." 2:14 ESV

"Now thanks be to God who always leads us in triumph in Christ, and through us diffuses the fragrance of His knowledge in every place. For we are to God the fragrance of Christ among those who are being saved and among those who are perishing." 2:14 NKJV

-Great to know and learn that in Christ we will always have victory! Always take heart and the power of prayer is great!

*"For the love of Christ compels us, because we judge thus; that if One died for all, then all died; and He died for all, that those who live should live no longer for themselves, but for Him who died for them and rose again." 5:14 NKJV

*"Therefore, if anyone is in Christ, he is a new creation. The old has passed away; behold, the new has come." 5:17 ESV

"Therefore, if anyone is in Christ, he is a new creation; old things have passed away; behold, all things have become new." 5:17 NKJV

*"that is, in Christ God was reconciling the world to Himself, not counting their trespasses against them, and entrusting to us the message of reconciliation. Therefore, we are ambassadors for Christ, God making His appeal through us. We implore you on behalf of Christ, be reconciled to God." 5:19 ESV

"that is, that God was in Christ reconciling the world to Himself, not imputing their trespasses to them, and has committed to us the word of reconciliation. Now then, we are ambassadors for Christ, as though God were pleading through us: we implore you on Christ's behalf, be reconciled to God." 5:19 NKJV

*"But as you excel in everything- in faith, in speech, in knowledge, in all earnestness, and in our love for you- see that you excel in this act of grace also." (generosity) 8:7 ESV

"But as you abound in everything- in faith, in speech, in knowledge, in all diligence, and in your love for us- see that you abound in this grace also." (generosity) 8:7 NKJV

*"The point is this: whoever sows sparingly will also reap sparingly, and whoever sows bountifully will also reap bountifully. Each one must give as he has decided in his heart, not reluctantly or under compulsion, for God loves a cheerful giver. And God is able to make all grace abound to you, so that having all sufficiency in all things at all times, you may abound in every good work. As it is written, "He has distributed freely, he has given to the poor, his righteousness endures forever." 9:6 ESV

"But this I say: he who sows sparingly will also reap sparingly, and he who sows bountifully will also reap bountifully. So, let each one give as he purposes in his heart, not grudgingly or of necessity; for God loves a cheerful giver." 9:6 NKJV

****"But He said to me, "My grace is sufficient for you, for my power is made perfect in weakness. "Therefore, I will boast even more gladly of my weaknesses, so that the power of Christ may rest upon me. For the sake of Christ, then, I am content with weaknesses, insults, hardships, persecutions, and calamities. For when I am weak, then I am strong." 12:9 ESV

"And He said to me, "My grace is sufficient for you, for My strength is made perfect in weakness." Therefore, most gladly I will rather boast in my infirmities, that the power of Christ may rest upon me. Therefore, I take pleasure in infirmities, in reproaches, in needs, in persecutions, in distresses, for Christ's sake. For when I am weak, then I am strong." 12:9 NKJV

*"He is not weak in dealing with you, but is powerful among you. For He was crucified in weakness, but lives by the power of God. For we also

are weak in Him, but in dealing with you we will live with Him by the power of God." 13:3 ESV

"For though He was crucified in weakness, yet He lives by the power of God. For we also are weak in Him, but we shall live with Him by the power of God toward you." 13:4 NKJV

*"Now I pray to God that you do no evil, not that we should appear approved, but that you should do what is honorable." 13:7 NKJV

*"Finally, brethren, farewell. Become complete. Be of good comfort, be of one mind, live in peace; and the God of love and peace will be with you." 13:11 NKJV

Galatians

*"Grace to you and peace from God our Father and the Lord Jesus Christ, who gave Himself for our sins to deliver us from the present evil age, according to the will of our God and Father, to whom be the glory forever and ever. Amen." 1:3 ESV

"Grace to you and peace from God the father and our Lord Jesus Christ, who gave Himself for our sins, that He might deliver us from this present evil age, according to the will of our God and Father, to whom be glory forever and ever." 1:3 NKJV

*"For am I now seeking the approval of man, or of God? If I were still trying to please man, I would not be a servant of Christ." 1:10 ESV

***"I have been crucified with Christ. It is no longer I who live, but Christ who lives in me." 2:20 ESV

"I have been crucified with Christ; it is no longer I who live, but Christ lives in me; and the life which I now live in the flesh I live by faith in the Son of God, who loved me and gave Himself for me." 2:20 NKJV

***"For freedom Christ has set us free; stand firm therefore, and do not submit again to a yoke of slavery." 5:1 ESV

"Stand fast therefore in the liberty by which Christ has made us free, and do not be entangled again with a yoke of bondage." 5:1 NKJV

*"For you were called to freedom, brothers. Only do not use your freedom as an opportunity for the flesh, but through love serve one another. For the whole law is fulfilled in one word: You shall love your neighbor as yourself." 5:13 ESV

"For you, brethren, have been called to liberty; only do not use liberty as an opportunity for the flesh, but through love serve one another. For all the law is fulfilled in one word, even in this: You shall love your neighbor as yourself." 5:13 NKJV

-Pretty simple =)

*"For the desires of the flesh are against the Spirit, and the desires of the Spirit are against the flesh." 5:17 ESV

"I say then: Walk in the Spirit, and you shall not fulfill the lust of the flesh. For the flesh lusts against the Spirit, and the Spirit against the flesh; and these are contrary to one another, so that you do not do the things that you wish. But if you are led by the Spirit, you are not under the law." 5:16 NKJV

***"But the fruit of the Spirit is love, joy, peace, patience, kindness, goodness, faithfulness, gentleness, self-control; against such things there is no law. And those who belong to Christ Jesus have crucified the flesh with its passions and desires." 5:22 ESV

"But the fruit of the Spirit is love, joy, peace, longsuffering, kindness, goodness, faithfulness, gentleness, self-control. Against such there is no law. And those who are Christ's have crucified the flesh with its passions and desires." 5:22 NKJV

-Love this!! Being able to do it is so great!

*"Brothers, if anyone is caught in any transgression, you who are spiritual should restore him in a spirit of gentleness. Keep watch on yourself, lest you too be tempted. Bear one another's burdens, and so fulfill the law of Christ." 6:1 ESV

"Brethren, if a man is overtaken in any trespass, you who are spiritual restore such a one in a spirit of gentleness, considering yourself lest you also be tempted. Bear one another's burdens, and so fulfill the law of Christ." 6:1 NKJV

-This is very true we are to edify one another always.

***"Do not be deceived: for whatever one sows, that will he also reap. For the one who sows to his own flesh will from the flesh reap corruption, but the one who sows to the Spirit will from the Spirit reap eternal life. And let us not grow weary of doing good, for in due season we will reap, if we do not give up." 6:7 ESV

"Do not be deceived; for whatever a man sows, that he will also reap. For he who sows to his flesh will of the flesh reap corruption, but he who sows to the Spirit will of the Spirit reap everlasting life. And let us not grow weary while doing good, for in due season we shall reap if we do not lose heart." 6:7 NKJV

Ephesians

*"In Him you also trusted, after you heard the word of truth, the gospel of your salvation; in whom also, having believed, you were sealed with the Holy Spirit of promise, who is the guarantee of our inheritance until the redemption of the purchased possession, to the praise of His glory." 1:13 NKJV

*"that the God of our Lord Jesus Christ, the Father of glory, may give to you the spirit of wisdom and revelation in the knowledge of Him, the eyes of your understanding being enlightened; that you may know what is the hope of His calling, what are the riches of the glory of His inheritance in the saints, and what is the exceeding greatness of His power toward us who believe, according to the working of His mighty power which He worked in Christ when He raised Him from the dead and seated Him at His right hand in the heavenly places, far above all principality and power and might and dominion." 1:17 NKJV

*"And you He made alive, who were dead in trespasses and sins, in which you once walked according to the course of this world, according to the prince of the power of the air, the spirit who now works in the sons of disobedience, among whom also we all once conducted ourselves in the lusts of our flesh." 2:1 NKJV

"And you were dead in the trespasses and sins in which you once walked, following the course of this world, following the prince of the power of the air, the spirit that is now at work in the sons of disobedience-among whom we all once lived in the passions of our flesh, carrying out the desires of the body and the mind, and were by nature children of wrath, like the rest of mankind. But God, being rich in mercy, because of the great love with which He loved us, even when we were dead in our trespasses, made us alive together with Christ- by grace you have been saved- and raised us up with Him and seated us with Him in the heavenly places in

Christ Jesus, so that in the coming ages he might show the immeasurable riches of his grace in kindness toward us in Christ Jesus." 2:1 ESV

*"For we are His workmanship, created in Christ Jesus for good works, which God prepared beforehand that we should walk in them." 2:10 NKJV

*"remember that you were at that time separated from Christ, alienated from the commonwealth of Israel and strangers to the covenants of promise, having no hope and without God in the world. But now in Christ Jesus you who once were far off have been brought near by the blood of Christ. For He Himself is our peace, who has made us both one and has broken down in His flesh the dividing wall of hostility by abolishing the law of commandments... and might reconcile us both to God in one body through the cross, thereby killing the hostility." 2:12 ESV

"that at that time you were without Christ, being aliens from the commonwealth of Israel and strangers from the covenants of promise, having no hope and without God in the world. But now in Christ Jesus you who once were far off have been brought near by the blood of Christ. For He Himself is our peace, who has made both one, and has broken down the middle wall of separation, having abolished in His flesh the enmity, that is, the law of commandments contained in ordinances, so as to create in Himself one new man from the two, thus making peace, and that he might reconcile them both to God in one body through the cross, thereby putting to death the enmity. And He came and preached peace to you who were afar off and to those who were near. For through Him we both have access by one Spirit to the Father." 2:12 NKJV

*"in whom we have boldness and access with confidence through our faith in Him. So, I ask you not to lose heart over what I am suffering for you, which is your glory." 3:12 ESV

"in whom we have boldness and access with confidence through faith in Him. Therefore, I ask that you do not lose heart at my tribulations for you, which is your glory." 3:12 NKJV

-*Important to know this well as you face many adversities.*

***"that according to the riches of his glory He may grant you to be strengthened with power through His Spirit in your inner being, so that Christ may dwell in your hearts through faith- that you, being rooted and grounded in love, may have strength to comprehend with all the saints what is the breadth and length and height and depth, and to know the love of Christ that surpasses knowledge, that you may be filled with all the fullness of God." 3:16 ESV

-AMEN!!

***"walk in a manner worthy of the calling to which you have been called, with all humility and gentleness, with patience, bearing with one another in love, eager to maintain the unity of the Spirit in the bond of peace." 4:1 ESV

"walk worthy of the calling with which you were called, with all lowliness and gentleness, with longsuffering, bearing with one another in love, endeavoring to keep the unity of the Spirit in the bond of peace." 4:1 NKJV

-So important to practice this =)

***"and to be renewed in the spirit of your minds, and to put on the new self, created after the likeness of God in true righteousness and holiness." 4:23 ESV

"be renewed in the spirit of your mind, and that you put on the new man which was created according to God, in true righteousness and holiness." 4:23 NKJV

-This is a practice that moves you forward.

***"Let no corrupting talk come out of your mouths, but only such as is good for building up, as fits the occasion, that it may give grace to those who hear." 4:29 ESV

"Let no corrupt word proceed out of your mouth, but what is good for necessary edification, that it may impart grace to the hearers." 4:29 NKJV

*"Be kind to one another, tenderhearted, forgiving one another, as God in Christ forgave you." 4:32 ESV

"And be kind to one another, tenderhearted, forgiving one another, even as God in Christ forgave you." 4:32 NKJV

*"Therefore, do not become partners with them; for at one time you were darkness, but now you are light in the Lord. Walk as children of light (for the fruit of light is found in all that is good and right and true)" 5:7 ESV

"For you were once darkness, but now you are light in the Lord. Walk as children of light (for the fruit of the Spirit is in all goodness, righteousness, and truth)" 5:8 NKJV

*"Look carefully then how you walk, not as unwise but as wise, making the best use of the time, because the days are evil." 5:15 ESV

*"Therefore, do not be unwise, but understand what the will of the Lord is. And do not be drunk with wine, in which is dissipation; but be filled with the Spirit." 5:17 NKJV

***"Finally, be strong in the Lord and in the strength of His might. Put on the whole armor of God, that you may be able to stand against the schemes of the devil. For we do not wrestle against flesh and blood, but against the rulers, against the authorities, against the cosmic powers over this present darkness, against the spiritual forces of evil in the heavenly places." 6:10 ESV

"Finally, my brethren, be strong in the Lord and in the power of His might. Put on the whole armor of God, that you may be able to stand against the wiles of the devil. For we do not wrestle against flesh and blood, but against principalities, against powers, against the rulers of the darkness of this age, against spiritual hosts of wickedness in the heavenly places. Therefore, take up the whole armor of God, that you may be able to withstand in the evil day, and having done all, to stand." 6:10 NKJV

***"Stand therefore, having fastened on the belt of truth. And having put on the breastplate of righteousness, and, as shoes for your feet, having put on the readiness given by the gospel of peace. In all circumstances take up the shield of faith, with which you can extinguish all the flaming darts of the evil one; and take the helmet of salvation, and the sword of the Spirit, which is the word of God, praying at all times in the Spirit, with all prayer and supplication. To that end keep alert with all perseverance, making supplication for all the saints." 6:14 ESV

Philippians

***"And I am sure of this, that He who began a good work in you will bring it to completion at the day of Jesus Christ." 1:6 ESV

"being confident of this very thing, that He who has begun a good work in you will complete it until the day of Jesus Christ." 1:6 NKJV

*"so that you may approve what is excellent, and so be pure and blameless for the day of Christ, filled with the fruit of righteousness that comes through Jesus Christ, to the glory and praise of God." 1:10 ESV

*"And most of the brothers, having become confident in the Lord by my imprisonment, are much more bold to speak the word without fear." 1:14 ESV

*"For me to live is Christ, and to die is gain." 1:21 ESV

***"Do nothing from selfish ambition or conceit, but in humility count others more significant than yourselves. Let each of you look not only to his own interests, but also to the interests of others. Have this mind among yourselves, which is yours in Christ Jesus, who, though He was in the form of God, did not count equality with God a thing to be grasped, but emptied Himself, by taking the form of a servant." 2:3 ESV

***"Do all things without grumbling or disputing, that you may be blameless and innocent, children of God without blemish in the midst of a crooked and twisted generation, among whom you shine as lights in the world, holding fast to the word of life, so that in the day of Christ I may be proud that I did not run in vain or labor in vain." 2:14 ESV

"Do all things without complaining and disputing, that you may become blameless and harmless, children of God without fault in the midst of a crooked and perverse generation, among whom you shine as lights in the world, holding fast the word of life, so that I may rejoice in the day of Christ that I have not run in vain or labored in vain." 2:14 NKJV

***"Not that I have already obtained this or am already perfect, but I press on to make it my own, because Christ Jesus has made me His own... But one thing I do: forgetting what lies behind and straining forward to what lies ahead, I press on toward the goal for the prize of the upward call of God in Christ Jesus." 3:12 ESV

"Not that I have already attained, or am already perfected; but I press on, that I may lay hold of that for which Christ Jesus has also laid hold of me. Brethren, I do not count myself to have apprehended; but one thing I do, forgetting those things which are behind and reaching forward to those things which are ahead, I press toward the goal for the prize of the upward call of God in Christ Jesus." 3:12 NKJV

***"Rejoice in the Lord always; again, I will say, rejoice. Let your reasonableness be known to everyone. The Lord is at hand; do not be anxious about anything, but in everything by prayer and supplication with thanksgiving let your requests be made known to God. And the peace of God, which surpasses all understanding, will guard your hearts and your minds in Christ Jesus. Finally, brothers, whatever is true, whatever is honorable, whatever is just, whatever is pure, whatever is lovely, whatever is commendable, if there is any excellence, if there is anything worthy of praise, think about these things. What you have learned and received and heard and seen in me- practice these things, and the God of peace will be with you." 4:4 ESV

***"I can do all things through Him who strengthens me." 4:13 ESV

"I can do all things through Christ who strengthens me." 4:13 NKJV

*"And my God will supply every need of yours according to His riches in glory in Christ Jesus. To our God and Father be glory forever and ever. Amen." 4:19 ESV

"And my God shall supply all your need according to His riches in glory by Christ Jesus. Now to our God and Father be glory forever and ever. Amen. "4:19 NKJV

Colossians

*"the gospel, which has come to you, as indeed in the whole world it is bearing fruit and increasing- as it also does among you, since the day you heard it and understood the grace of God in truth." 1:6 ESV

***"so as to walk in a manner worthy of the Lord, fully pleasing to Him, bearing fruit in every good work and increasing in the knowledge of God. May you be strengthened with all power, according to His glorious might, for all endurance and patience with joy, giving thanks to the Father, who has qualified you to share in the inheritance of the saints in light." 1:10 ESV

"that you may walk worthy of the Lord, fully pleasing Him, being fruitful in every good work and increasing in the knowledge of God; strengthened with all might, according to His glorious power, for all patience and longsuffering with joy; giving thanks to the Father who has qualified us to be partakers of the inheritance of the saints in the light. He has delivered us from the power of darkness and conveyed us into the kingdom of the Son of His love, in whom we have redemption through His blood, the forgiveness of sins." 1:10 NKJV

*"if indeed you continue in the faith, stable and steadfast, not shifting from the hope of the gospel that you heard." 1:23 ESV

"in the body of His flesh through death, to present you holy, and blameless, and above reproach in His sight- if indeed you continue in the faith, grounded and steadfast, and are not moved away from the hope of the gospel which you heard." 1:22 NKJV

*"the mystery hidden for ages and generations but now revealed to His saints. To them God chose to make known how great among the gentiles are the riches of the glory of this mystery, which is Christ in you, the hope of glory. Him we proclaim, warning everyone and teaching everyone with all wisdom, that we may present everyone mature in Christ." 1:26 ESV

"the mystery which has been hidden from ages and from generations, but now has been revealed to His saints. To them God willed to make known what are the riches of the glory of this mystery among the gentiles: which is Christ in you, the hope of glory. Him we preach, warning every man and teaching every man in all wisdom, that we may present every man perfect in Christ Jesus." 1:26 NKJV

*"that their hearts may be encouraged, being knit together in love, to reach all the riches of full assurance of understanding and the knowledge of God's mystery, which is Christ." 2:2 ESV

***"Therefore, as you received Christ Jesus the Lord, so walk in Him, rooted and built up in Him and established in the faith, just as you were taught, abounding in thanksgiving." 2:6 ESV

"As you therefore have received Christ Jesus the Lord, so walk in Him, rooted and built up in Him and established in the faith, as you have been taught, abounding in it with thanksgiving. Beware lest anyone cheat you through philosophy and empty deceit, according to the tradition of men, according to the basic principles of the world, and not according to Christ. For in Him dwells all the fullness of the Godhead bodily; and you are complete in Him, who is the head of all principality and power." 2:6 NKJV

*"And you, who were dead in your trespasses and the uncircumcision of your flesh, God made alive together with Him, having forgiven us all our trespasses, by canceling the record of debt that stood against us with its legal demands. This He set aside, nailing it to the cross. He disarmed the rulers and authorities and put them to open shame, by triumphing over them in Him." 2:13 ESV

"And you, being dead in your trespasses and the uncircumcision of your flesh of your flesh, He has made alive together with Him, having forgiven you all trespasses, having wiped out the handwriting of requirements that was against us, which was contrary to us. And He has taken it out of the way, having nailed it to the cross. Having disarmed principalities and powers, He made a public spectacle of them, triumphing over them in it." 2:13 NKJV

****"Put on then, as God's chosen ones, holy and beloved, compassionate hearts, kindness, humility, meekness, and patience, bearing with one another and, if one has a complaint against another, forgiving each other; as the Lord has forgiven you, so you also must forgive. And above all these put-on love, which binds everything together in perfect harmony." 3:12 ESV

"Therefore, as the elect of God, holy and beloved, put on tender mercies, kindness, humility, meekness, longsuffering; bearing with one another, and forgiving one another, if anyone has a complaint against another; even as Christ forgave you, so you also must do. But above all these things put on love, which is the bond of perfection. And let the peace of God rule in your hearts, to which also you were called in one body; and be thankful. Let the word of Christ dwell in you richly in all wisdom, teaching and admonishing one another." 3:12 NKJV

*"And whatever you do, in word or deed, do everything in the name of the Lord Jesus, giving thanks to God the Father through Him." 3:17 ESV

*"Whatever you do, work heartily, as for the Lord and not for men, knowing that from the Lord you will receive the inheritance as your reward." 3:23 ESV

*"But he who does wrong will be repaid for what he has done, and there is no partiality." 3:25 NKJV

*"Continue steadfastly in prayer, being watchful in it with thanksgiving." 4:2 ESV

"Continue earnestly in prayer, being vigilant in it with thanksgiving." 4:2 NKJV

*"Walk in wisdom toward outsiders, making the best use of the time. Let your speech always be gracious, seasoned with salt, so that you may know how you ought to answer each person." 4:5 ESV

"Walk in wisdom toward those who are outside, redeeming the time. Let your speech always be with grace, seasoned with salt, that you may know how you ought to answer each one." 4:5 NKJV

1 Thessalonians

*"but just as we have been approved by God to be entrusted with the gospel, so we speak, not to please man, but to please God who tests our hearts." 2:4 ESV

"But as we have been approved by God to be entrusted with the gospel, even so we speak, not as pleasing men, but God who tests our hearts." 2:4 NKJV

*"For you know how, like a father with his children, we exhorted each one of you and encouraged you and charged you to walk in a manner worthy of God, who calls you into His own kingdom and glory." 2:11 ESV

"as you know how we exhorted, and comforted, and charged every one of you, as a father does his own children, that you would walk worthy of God who calls you into His own kingdom and glory." 2:11 NKJV

*"... to establish you and encourage you concerning your faith, that no one should be shaken by these afflictions; for you yourselves know that we are appointed to this. For, in fact, we told you before when we were with you that you would suffer tribulation." 3:2 NKJV

*"and may the Lord make you increase and abound in love for one another and for all, as we do for you, so that He may establish your hearts blameless in holiness before our God and Father, at the coming of our Lord Jesus with all His saints." 3:12 ESV

*"For you know what instructions we gave you through the Lord Jesus. For this is the will of God, your sanctification: that you abstain from sexual immorality; that each one of you know how to control his own body in holiness and honor, not in the passion of lust like the gentiles who do not know God." 4:2 ESV

"For this is the will of God, your sanctification: that you should abstain from sexual immorality; that each of you should know how to possess his own vessel in sanctification and honor, not in passion of lust, like the gentiles who do not know God." 4:3 NKJV

*"Now concerning brotherly love you have no need for anyone to write to you, for you yourselves have been taught by God to love one another, for that indeed is what you are doing to all the brothers throughout Macedonia. But we urge you, brothers, to do this more and more, and to aspire to live quietly, and to mind your own affairs, and to work with your

hands, as we instructed you, so that you may walk properly before outsiders and be dependent on no one." 4:9 ESV

"... but we urge you, brethren, that you increase more and more; that you also aspire to lead a quiet life, to mind your own business, and to work with your own hands, as we commanded you, that you may walk properly toward those who are outside, and that you may lack nothing." 4:10 NKJV

*"But you, brethren, are not in darkness, so that this day should overtake you as a thief. You are all sons of light and sons of the day. We are not of the night nor of darkness. Therefore, let us not sleep, as others do, but let us watch and be sober." 5:4 NKJV

****"But since we belong to the day, let us be sober, having put on the breastplate of faith and love, and for a helmet the hope of salvation. For God has not destined us for wrath, but to obtain salvation through our Lord Jesus Christ, who died for us so that whether we are awake or sleep we might live with Him. Therefore encourage one another and build one another up." 5:8 ESV

***"And we urge you, brothers, admonish the idle, encourage the fainthearted, help the weak, be patient with them all." 5:14 ESV

"Now we exhort you, brethren, warn those who are unruly, comfort the fainthearted, uphold the weak, be patient with all. See that no one renders evil for evil to anyone, but always pursue what is good both for yourselves and for all. Rejoice always, pray without ceasing, in everything give thanks; for this is the will of God in Christ Jesus for you." 5:14 NKJV

*"but test everything; hold fast what is good. Abstain from every form of evil." 5:21 ESV

2 Thessalonians

***"not to be quickly shaken in mind or alarmed, either by a spirit or a spoken word, or a letter seeming to be from us, to the effect that the day of the Lord has come." 2:2 ESV

-It's not over until we make it.

*"for those who are perishing, because they refused to love the truth and so be saved." 2:10 ESV

"and with all unrighteous deception among those who perish, because they did not receive the love of the truth, that they might be saved." 2:10 NKJV

*"Now may our Lord Jesus Christ Himself, and our God and Father, who has loved us and given us everlasting consolation and good hope by grace, comfort your hearts and establish you in every good word and work." 2:16 NKJV

=)

*"and that we may be delivered from wicked and evil men. For not all have faith. But the Lord is faithful. He will establish you and guard you against the evil one." 3:2 ESV

"and that we may be delivered from unreasonable and wicked men; for not all have faith. But the Lord is faithful, who will establish you and guard you from the evil one." 3:2 NKJV

PRAISE YOU LORD

***"May the Lord direct your hearts to the love of God and to the steadfastness of Christ." 3:5 ESV

"Now may the Lord direct your hearts into the love of God and into the patience of Christ." 3:5 NKJV

-This is one of the most awesome gifts man can receive.

*"For you yourselves know how you ought to imitate us, because we were not idle when we were with you, nor did we eat anyone's bread without paying for it, but with toil and labor we worked night and day, that we might not be a burden to any of you. It was not because we did not have that right, but to give you in ourselves an example to imitate." 3:7 ESV

*"Now such persons we command and encourage in the Lord Jesus Christ to do their work quietly and to earn their own living." 3:12 ESV

1 Timothy

***"The aim of our charge is love that issues from a pure heart and a good conscience and a sincere faith." 1:5 ESV

"... teach no other doctrine, nor give heed to fables and endless genealogies, which cause disputes rather than godly edification which is in faith. Now the purpose of the commandment is love from a pure heart, from a good conscience, and from sincere faith." 1:3 NKJV

*"for kings and all who are in high positions, that we may lead a peaceful and quiet life, godly and dignified in every way. This is good, and it is pleasing in the sight of God our savior, who desires all people to be saved and to come to the knowledge of the truth. For there is one God, and there is one mediator between God and men, the man Christ Jesus." 2:2 ESV

"for kings and all who are in authority, that we may lead a quiet and peaceable life in all godliness and reverence. For this is good and acceptable in the sight of God our savior, who desires all men to be saved and to come to the knowledge of the truth. For there is one God and one Mediator between God and men, the man Christ Jesus, who gave himself a ransom for all." 2:2 NKJV

*"Great indeed, we confess, is the mystery of godliness: He was manifested in the flesh, vindicated by the Spirit, seen by angels, proclaimed among the nations, believed on in the world, taken up in glory." 3:16 ESV

*"For everything created by God is good, and nothing is to be rejected if it is received with thanksgiving." 4:4 ESV

*"Have nothing to do with irreverent, silly myths. Rather train yourself for godliness; for while bodily training is of some value, godliness is of value in every way, as it holds promise for the present life and also for the life to come. The saying is trustworthy and deserving of full acceptance. For to this end we toil and strive, because we have our hope set on the living God, who is the savior of all people, especially of those who believe." 4:7 ESV

"But reject profane and old wives fables and exercise yourself toward godliness. For bodily exercise profits a little, but godliness is profitable for all things, having promise of the life that now is and of that which is to come. This is a faithful saying and worthy of all acceptance. For to this end we both labor and suffer reproach, because we trust in the living God, who is the savior of all men, especially of those who believe." 4:7 NKJV

*"Let no one despise you for your youth, but set the believers an example in speech, in conduct, in love, in faith, in purity." 4:12 ESV

"Let no one despise your youth, but be an example to the believers in word, in conduct, in love, in spirit, in faith, in purity." 4:12 NKJV

*"Do not neglect the gift you have, which was given you by prophesy when the council of elders laid their hands on you. Practice these things,

immerse yourself in them, so that all may see your progress. Keep a close watch on yourself and on the teaching. Persist in this, for by so doing you will save both yourself and your hearers." 4:14 ESV

"Do not neglect the gift that is in you, which was given to you by prophesy with the laying on of the hands of the eldership. Meditate on these things; give yourself entirely to them, that your progress may be evident to all. Take heed to yourself and to the doctrine. Continue in them, for in doing this you will save both yourself and those who hear you." 4:14 NKJV

*"Do not rebuke an older man but encourage him as you would a father, younger men as brothers, older women as mothers, younger women as sisters in all purity." 5:1 ESV

"Do not rebuke an older man, but exhort him as a father, younger men as brothers, older women as mothers, younger women as sisters, with all purity." 5:1 NKJV

- *Love this*

*"But godliness with contentment is great gain, for we brought nothing into the world, and we cannot take anything out of the world. But if we have food and clothing, with these we will be content. But those who desire to be rich fall into temptation, into a snare, into many senseless and harmful desires that plunge people into ruin and destruction. For the love of money is a root of all kinds of evils." 6:6 ESV

"Now godliness with contentment is great gain. For we brought nothing into this world, and it is certain we can carry nothing out. And having food and clothing, with these we shall be content. But those who desire to be rich fall into temptation and a snare, and into many foolish and harmful lusts which drown men in destruction and perdition. For the love of money is a root of all kinds of evil, for which some have strayed from the faith in their greediness, and pierced themselves through with many sorrows." 6:6 NKJV

***"But as for you, O man of God, flee these things. Pursue righteousness, godliness, faith, love, steadfastness, gentleness. Fight the good fight of the faith. Take hold of the eternal life to which you were called and about which you made the good confession in the presence of many witnesses." 6:11 ESV

"But you, O man of God, flee these things and pursue righteousness, godliness, faith, love, patience, gentleness. Fight the good fight of faith, lay hold on eternal life, to which you were also called and have confessed the good confession in the presence of many witnesses. I urge you in the sight of God who gives life to all things, and before Christ Jesus who witnessed the good confession before Pontius Pilate, that you keep the commandment without spot, blameless until our Lord Jesus Christ's appearing." 6:11 NKJV

*"As for the rich in this present age, charge them not to be haughty, nor to set their hopes on the uncertainty of riches, but on God, who richly provides us with everything to enjoy. They are to do good, to be rich in good works, to be generous and ready to share, thus storing up treasure for themselves as a good foundation for the future, so that they may take hold of that which is truly life." 6:17 ESV

"Command those who are rich in this present age not to be haughty, nor to trust in uncertain riches but in the living God, who gives us richly all things to enjoy. Let them do good, that they be rich in good works, ready to give, willing to share, storing up for themselves a good foundation for the time to come, that they may lay hold on eternal life." 6:17 NKJV

2 Timothy

*"for God gave us a spirit not of fear but of power and love and self-control. Therefore do not be ashamed of the testimony about our Lord, nor of me His prisoner, but share in suffering for the gospel by the power of God, who saved us and called us to a holy calling, not because of our works but because of His own purpose and grace, which He gave us in Christ Jesus before the ages began, and which now has been manifested through the appearing of our Savior Christ Jesus, who abolished death and brought life and immortality to light through the gospel." 1:7 ESV

"For God has not given us a spirit of fear, but of power and of love and of a sound mind." 1:7 NKJV

*"who has saved us and called us with a holy calling, not according to our works, but according to His own purpose and grace which was given to us in Christ Jesus before time began; but has now been revealed by the

appearing of our Savior Jesus Christ, who has abolished death and brought life and immortality to light through the gospel." 1:9 NKJV

***"You therefore my son, be strong in the grace that is in Christ Jesus." 2:1 NKJV

***"Share in suffering as a good soldier of Christ Jesus. No soldier gets entangled in civilian pursuits, since his aim is to please the one who enlisted him. An athlete is not crowned unless he competes according to the rules. It is the hard-working farmer who ought to have the first share of the crops. Think over what I say, for the Lord will give you understanding in everything." 2:3 ESV

"You therefore must endure hardship as a good soldier of Jesus Christ. No one engaged in warfare entangles himself with the affairs of this life, that he may please the one who enlisted him as a soldier. And, if anyone competes in athletics, he is not crowned unless he competes according to the rules." 2:3 NKJV

*"The saying is trustworthy, for: If we have died with Him, we will also live with Him; if we endure, we will also reign with Him; if we deny Him, He also will deny us; if we are faithless, He remains faithful- for He cannot deny Himself." 2:11 ESV

"This is a faithful saying: For if we died with Him, we shall also live with Him. If we endure, we shall also reign with Him. If we deny Him, He also will deny us. If we are faithless, He remains faithful; He cannot deny Himself." 2:11 NKJV

***"Do your best to present yourself to God as one approved, a worker who has no need to be ashamed, rightly handling the word of truth." 2:15 ESV

"Be diligent to present yourself approved to God, a worker who does not need to be ashamed, rightly dividing the word of truth. But shun profane and idle babblings, for they will increase to more ungodliness." 2:15 NKJV

*"But God's firm foundation stands, bearing this seal: The Lord knows those who are His, and, let everyone who names the name of the Lord depart from iniquity." 2:19 ESV

"Nevertheless, the solid foundation of God stands, having this seal: The Lord knows those who are His, and let everyone who names the name of Christ depart from iniquity." 2:19 NKJV

*"Therefore, if anyone cleanses himself from what is dishonorable, he will be a vessel for honorable use, set apart as holy, useful to the Master of the house, ready for every good work. So, flee youthful passions and pursue righteousness, faith, love, and peace, along with those who call on the Lord from a pure heart." 2:21 ESV

"Therefore, if anyone cleanses himself from the latter, he will be a vessel for honor, sanctified and useful for the Master, prepared for every good work. Flee also youthful lusts; but pursue righteousness, faith, love, peace with those who call on the Lord out of a pure heart." 2:21 NKJV

*"And the Lord's servant must not be quarrelsome but kind to everyone, able to teach, patiently enduring evil, correcting his opponents with gentleness." 2:24 ESV

"And a servant of the Lord must not quarrel but be gentle to all, able to teach, patient, in humility correcting those who are in opposition." 2:24 NKJV

*"But understand this, that in the last days there will come times of difficulty." 3:1 ESV

"But know this, that in the last days perilous times will come. For men will be lovers of themselves, lovers of money, boasters, proud, blasphemers, disobedient to parents, unthankful, unholy, unloving, unforgiving, slanderers, without self-control, brutal, despisers of good, traitors, lovers of pleasure rather than lovers of God. And from such people turn away!" 3:1 NKJV

*"Indeed, all who desire to live a godly life in Christ Jesus will be persecuted, while evil people and impostors will go on from bad to worse." 3:12 ESV

"Yes, and all who desire to live godly in Christ Jesus will suffer persecution." 3:12 NKJV

*"But as for you, continue in what you have learned and have firmly believed, knowing from whom you learned it and how from childhood you have been acquainted with the sacred writings, which are able to make you wise for salvation through faith in Christ Jesus." 3:14 ESV

*"All scripture is breathed out by God and profitable for teaching, for reproof, for correction, for the training in righteousness, that the man of God may be complete, equipped for every good work." 3:16 ESV

"All scripture is given by inspiration of God, and is profitable for doctrine, for reproof, for correction, for instruction in righteousness, that the man of God may be complete, thoroughly equipped for every good work." 3:16 NKJV

*"As for you, always be sober minded, endure suffering, do the work of an evangelist, fulfill your ministry." 4:5 ESV

"But you be watchful in all things, endure afflictions, do the work of an evangelist, fulfill your ministry." 4:5 NKJV

*"I have fought the good fight, I have finished the race, I have kept the faith." 4:7 ESV

"I have fought the good fight, I have finished the race, I have kept the faith." 4:7 NKJV

*"But the Lord stood by me and strengthened me, so that through me the message might be fully proclaimed and all the gentiles might hear it. So, I was rescued from the lion's mouth. The Lord will rescue me from every evil deed and bring me safely into His heavenly kingdom. To Him be glory forever and ever! Amen!" 4:17 ESV

"But the Lord stood with me and strengthened me, so that the message might be preached fully through me, and that all the gentiles might hear. Also, I was delivered out of the mouth of the lion. And the Lord will deliver me from every evil work and preserve me for His heavenly kingdom. To Him be glory forever and ever! Amen!" 4:17 NKJV

Titus

*"Older men are to be sober-minded, dignified, self-controlled, sound in faith, in love, and in steadfastness." 2:2 ESV

*"For the grace of God has appeared, bringing salvation for all people, training us to renounce ungodliness and worldly passions, and to live self-controlled, upright and godly lives in the present age." 2:11 ESV

"For the grace of God that brings salvation has appeared to all men, teaching us that, denying ungodliness and worldly lusts, we should live soberly, righteously, and godly in the present age, looking for the blessed hope and glorious appearing of our great God and Savior Jesus Christ, who gave Himself for us, that He might redeem us from every lawless deed and purify for Himself His own special people, zealous for good works." 2:11 NKJV

*"Remind them to be submissive to rulers and authorities, to be obedient, to be ready for every good work, to speak evil of no one, to avoid quarreling, to be gentle, and to show perfect courtesy toward all people." 3:1 ESV

"Remind them to be subject to rulers and authorities, to obey, to be ready for every good work, to speak evil of no one, to be peaceable, gentle, showing all humility to all men." 3:1 NKJV

*"But when the kindness and the love of God our Savior toward man appeared, not by works of righteousness which we have done, but according to His mercy He saved us, through the washing of regeneration and renewing of the Holy Spirit." 3:4 ESV

Philemon

*"and I pray that the sharing of your faith may become effective for the full knowledge of every good thing that is in us for the sake of Christ." 1:6 ESV

*"Yes, brother, let me have joy from you in the Lord; refresh my heart in the Lord." 1:20 ESV

Hebrews

***"Long ago, at many times and in many ways, God spoke to our fathers by the prophets, but in these last days He has spoken to us by His Son, whom He appointed the heir of all things, through whom also He created the world. He is the radiance of the glory of God and the exact imprint of His nature, and He upholds the universe by the word of His power." 1:1 ESV

"has in these last days spoken to us by His Son, whom He has appointed heir of all things, through whom also He made the worlds; who being the brightness of His glory and the express image of His person, and upholding all things by the word of His power, when He had by Himself purged our sins, sat down at the right hand of the majesty on high." 1:2 NKJV

*"For it was fitting that He, for whom and by whom all things exist, in bringing many sons to glory, should make the founder of their salvation perfect through suffering. For He who sanctifies and those who are sanctified all have one source." 2:10 ESV

"For it was fitting for Him, for whom are all things and by whom are all things, in bringing many sons to glory, to make the captain of their salvation perfect through sufferings. For both He who sanctifies and those who are being sanctified are all of one, for which reason He is not ashamed to call them brethren." 2:10 NKJV

*"Therefore, He had to be made like His brothers in every respect, so that He might become a merciful and faithful high priest in the service of God, to make propitiation for the sins of the people. For because He Himself has suffered when tempted, He is able to help those who are being tempted." 2:17 ESV

*"Since then we have a great high priest who has passed through the heavens, Jesus, the Son of God, let us hold fast our confession. For we do not have a high priest who is unable to sympathize with our weaknesses, but one who in every respect has been tempted as we are, yet without sin. Let us then with confidence draw near to the throne of grace, that we may receive mercy and find grace to help in time of need." 4:14 ESV

*"And being made perfect, He became the source of eternal salvation to all who obey Him." 5:9 ESV

"And having been perfected, He became the author of eternal salvation to all who obey Him." 5:9 NKJV

*"For God is not unjust so as to overlook your work and the love that you have shown for His name in serving the saints, as you still do. And we desire each one of you to show the same earnestness to have the full assurance of hope until the end, so that you may not be sluggish, but imitators of those who through faith and patience inherit the promises." 6:10 ESV

*"(For the law made nothing perfect); but on the other hand, a better hope is introduced, through which we draw near to God." 7:19 ESV

"For the law made nothing perfect; on the other hand, there is the bringing in of a better hope, through which we draw near to God." 7:19 NKJV

*"But He holds His priesthood permanently, because He continues forever. Consequently, He is able to save to the uttermost those who draw near to God through Him, since He always lives to make intercession for them." 7:24 ESV

"But He, because He continues forever, has an unchangeable priesthood. Therefore, He is also able to save to the uttermost those who come to God through Him, since He always lives to make intercession for them. For such a High Priest was fitting for us, who is holy, harmless, undefiled, separate from sinners, and has become higher than the heavens." 7:24 NKJV

***"For this is the covenant that I will make with the house of Israel after those days, declares the Lord: I will put My laws into their minds, and write them on their hearts, and I will be their God, and they shall be my people. And they shall not teach, each one his neighbor and each one his brother, saying, 'Know the Lord,' for they shall all know Me, from the least of them to the greatest. For I will be merciful toward their iniquities, and I will remember their sins no more." 8:10 ESV

*"In that He says, "A new covenant," He has made the first obsolete." 8:13 NKJV

*"For it is impossible for the blood of bulls and goats to take away sins." 10:4 ESV

*"But when Christ had offered for all time a single sacrifice for sins, He sat down at the right hand of God, waiting from that time until His enemies should be made a footstool for His feet. For by a single offering He has perfected for all time those who are being sanctified." 10:12 ESV

*"This is the covenant that I will make with them after those days, declares the Lord: I will put My laws on their hearts, and write them on their minds," then He adds, "I will remember their sins and their lawless deeds no more." 10:16 ESV

"This is the covenant that I will make with them after those days, says the Lord: I will put my laws into their hearts, and in their minds I will write them." 10:16 NKJV

*"Let us draw near with a true heart in full assurance of faith, with our hearts sprinkled clean from an evil conscience and our bodies washed with pure water. Let us hold fast the confession of our hope without wavering, for He who promised is faithful." 10:22 ESV

"Therefore, brethren, having boldness to enter the Holiest by the blood of Jesus, by a new and living way which He consecrated for us, through the veil, that is, His flesh, and having a High Priest over the house of God, let us draw near with a true heart in full assurance of faith, having our hearts sprinkled from an evil conscience and our bodies washed with pure water." 10:19 NKJV

*"And let us consider how to stir up one another to love and good works, not neglecting to meet together, as is the habit of some, but encouraging one another, and all the more as you see the day drawing near. For if we go on sinning deliberately after receiving the knowledge of the truth, there no longer remains a sacrifice for sins, but a fearful expectation of judgment, and a fury of fire that will consume the adversaries." 10:24 ESV

"And let us consider one another in order to stir up love and good works, not forsaking the assembly of ourselves together, as is the manner of some, but exhorting one another, and so much the more as you see the day approaching." 10:24 NKJV

*"Therefore, do not throw away your confidence, which has a great reward. For you have need of endurance, so that when you have done the will of God you may receive what is promised." 10:35 ESV

"Therefore, do not cast away your confidence, which has great reward. For you have need of endurance, so that after you have done the will of God, you may receive the promise." 10:35 NKJV

*"But we are not of those who shrink back and are destroyed, but of those who have faith and preserve their souls." 10:39 ESV

-*Don't fear this but be still and know you are being made stronger no matter how difficult life is. You should light up in darkness and grow in the peace of God. You should face every thought and correct it with faith.*

*"And without faith it is impossible to please Him, for whoever would draw near to God must believe that He exists and that He rewards those who seek Him." 11:6 ESV

-*Faith is an action. It is choosing to keep going. Things will be very hard but walk in the love and trust power of God. Know your being made into something very precious to God and follow Him. Be still and mighty! Fortify your mind and let your spirit shine in peace. You are being transformed.*

***"And have you forgotten the exhortation that addresses you as sons? My son, do not regard lightly the discipline of the Lord, nor be weary when reproved by Him. For the Lord disciplines the one He loves, and chastises every son whom He receives." 12:5 ESV

"And you have forgotten the exhortation which speaks to you as to sons: My son, do not despise the chastening of the Lord, Nor be discouraged when you are rebuked by Him; For whom the Lord loves He chastens, and scourges every son whom He receives." 12:5 NKJV

***"For the moment all discipline seems painful rather than pleasant, but later it yields the peaceful fruit of righteousness to those who have been trained by it." 12:11 ESV

"Now no chastening seems to be joyful for the present, but painful; nevertheless, afterward it yields the peaceable fruit of righteousness to those who have been trained by it." 12:11 NKJV

-We all will experience these things, but knowing and having hope in this truth is very important.

*"Strive for peace with everyone, and for the holiness without which no one will see the Lord. See to it that no one fails to obtain the grace of God." 12:14 ESV

"Pursue peace with all people, and holiness, without which no one will see the Lord." 12:14 NKJV

*"Therefore, let us be grateful for receiving a kingdom that cannot be shaken, and thus let us offer to God acceptable worship, with reverence and awe, for our God is a consuming fire." 12:28 ESV

"Therefore, since we are receiving a kingdom which cannot be shaken, let us have grace, by which we may serve God acceptably with reverence and godly fear. For our God is a consuming fire." 12:28 NKJV

*"Let brotherly love continue. Do not neglect to show hospitality to strangers." 13:1 ESV

*"Remember those who are in prison, as though in prison with them, and those who are mistreated, since you also are in the body." 13:3 ESV

"Remember the prisoners as if chained with them- those who are mistreated- since you yourselves are in the body also." 13:3 NKJV

*"Keep your life free from the love of money, and be content with what you have, for He has said, "I will never leave you nor forsake you." So, we can confidently say, "The Lord is my helper; I will not fear; what can man do to me?" 13:5 ESV

"Let your conduct be without covetousness; be content with such things as you have. For He himself has said, "I will never leave you nor forsake you." So, we may boldly say: "The Lord is my helper; I will not fear. What can man do to me?" 13:5 NKJV

*"For here we have no lasting city, but we seek the city that is to come. Through Him then let us continually offer up a sacrifice of praise to God, that is, the fruit of lips that acknowledge His name. Do not neglect to do good and to share what you have, for such sacrifices are pleasing to God." 13:14 ESV

"Therefore, by Him let us continually offer the sacrifice of praise to God, that is, the fruit of our lips, giving thanks to His name. But do not forget to do good and to share, for with such sacrifices God is well pleased." 13:15 NKJV

*"Pray for us, for we are sure that we have a clear conscience, desiring to act honorably in all things." 13:18 ESV

"Pray for us; for we are confident that we have a good conscience, in all things desiring to live honorably." 13:18 NKJV

*"Now may the God of peace who brought again from the dead our Lord Jesus, the great shepherd of the sheep, by the blood of the eternal covenant, equip you with everything good that you may do His will, working in us that which is pleasing in His sight, through Jesus Christ, to whom be glory forever and ever. Amen!" 13:20 ESV

"Now may the God of peace who brought up our Lord Jesus from the dead, that great Shepherd of the sheep, through the blood of the everlasting covenant, make you complete in every good work to do His will, working in you what is well pleasing in His sight, through Jesus Christ, to whom be glory forever and ever. Amen!" 13:20 NKJV

James

*"Count it all joy, my brothers, when you meet trials of various kinds, for you know that the testing of your faith produces steadfastness. And let steadfastness have its full effect, that you may be perfect and complete, lacking in nothing. If any of you lacks wisdom, let Him ask God, who gives generously to all without reproach, and it will be given him." 1:2 ESV

"My brethren, count it all joy when you fall into various trials, knowing that the testing of your faith produces patience. But let patience have its perfect work, that you may be perfect and complete, lacking nothing. If any of you lacks wisdom, let him ask God, who gives to all liberally and without reproach, and it will be given to him." 1:2 NKJV

*"Blessed is the man who remains steadfast under trial, for when he has stood the test, he will receive the crown of life, which God has promised to those who love Him." 1:12 ESV

"Blessed is the man who endures temptation; for when he has been approved, he will receive the crown of life which the Lord has promised to those who love Him." 1:12 NKJV

*"Know this, my beloved brothers: let every person be quick to hear, slow to speak, slow to anger; for the anger of man does not produce the righteousness of God." 1:19 ESV

"So then, my beloved brethren, let every man be swift to hear, slow to speak, slow to wrath; for the wrath of man does not produce the righteousness of God." 1:19 NKJV

*"Therefore, put away all filthiness and rampant wickedness and receive with meekness the implanted word, which is able to save your souls." 1:21 ESV

"Therefore, lay aside all filthiness and overflow of wickedness, and receive with meekness the implanted word, which is able to save your souls." 1:21 NKJV

***"If you really fulfill the royal law according to the scripture, "You shall love your neighbor as yourself," you are doing well." 2:8 ESV

*"For judgment is without mercy to one who has shown no mercy. Mercy triumphs over judgment." 2:13 ESV

"For judgment is without mercy to one who has shown no mercy. Mercy triumphs over judgment." 2:13 NKJV

***"For we all stumble in many ways. And if anyone does not stumble in what he says, he is a perfect man, able also to bridle his whole body." 3:2 ESV

"For we all stumble in many things. If anyone does not stumble in word, he is a perfect man, able also to bridle the whole body." 3:2 NKJV

*"Who is wise and understanding among you? By his good conduct let him show his works in the meekness of wisdom." 3:13 ESV

*"For where jealousy and selfish ambition exist, there will be disorder and every vile practice. But the wisdom from above is first pure, then peaceable, gentle, open to reason, full of mercy and good fruits, impartial and sincere. And a harvest of righteousness is sown in peace by those who make peace." 3:16 ESV

"For where envy and self-seeking exist, confusion and every evil thing are there. But the wisdom that is from above is first pure, then peaceable, gentle, willing to yield, full of mercy and good fruits, without partiality and without hypocrisy. Now the fruit of righteousness is sown in peace by those who make peace." 3:16 NKJV

*"You ask and do not receive, because you ask wrongly, to spend it on your passions." 4:3 ESV

***"Submit yourselves therefore to God. Resist the devil, and he will flee from you. Draw near to God and He will draw near to you. Cleanse your hands, you sinners, and purify your hearts." 4:7 ESV

"Therefore, submit to God. Resist the devil and he will flee from you. Draw near to God and He will draw near to you. Cleanse your hands, you sinners, and purify your hearts, you double-minded... Humble yourselves in the sight of the Lord, and He will lift you up." 4:7 NKJV

*"There is only one Lawgiver and Judge, He who is able to save and to destroy. But who are you to judge your neighbor?" 4:12 ESV

"There is one Lawgiver, who is able to save and to destroy. Who are you to judge another?" 4:12 NKJV

*"You also, be patient. Establish your hearts, for the coming of the Lord is at hand." 5:8 ESV

"You also be patient. Establish your hearts, for the coming of the Lord is at hand." 5:8 NKJV

*"But above all, my brothers, do not swear, either by heaven or by earth or by any other oath, but let your 'yes' be yes and your 'no' be no, so that you may not fall under condemnation." 5:12 ESV

"But above all, my brethren, do not swear, either by heaven or by earth or with any other oath. But let your 'yes' be yes, and your 'no' no, lest you fall into judgment." 5:12 NKJV

*"Is anyone among you suffering? Let him pray. Is anyone cheerful? Let him sing praise." 5:13 ESV

*"And the prayer of faith will save the one who is sick, and the Lord will raise him up. And if he has committed sins, he will be forgiven. Therefore, confess your sins to one another and pray for one another, that you may be healed. The prayer of a righteous person has great power as it is working." 5:15 ESV

"And the prayer of faith will save the sick, and the Lord will raise him up. And if he has committed sins, he will be forgiven. Confess your trespasses to one another, and pray for one another, that you may be healed. The effective, fervent prayer of a righteous man avails much." 5:15 NKJV

*"My brothers, if anyone among you wanders from the truth and someone brings him back, let him know that whoever brings back a sinner from his wandering will save his soul from death and will cover a multitude of sins." 5:19 ESV

"Brethren, if anyone among you wanders from the truth, and someone turns him back, let him know that he who turns a sinner from the error of his way will save a soul from death and cover a multitude of sins." 5:19 NKJV

1 Peter

*"In this you rejoice, though now for a little while, if necessary, you have been grieved by various trials, so that the tested genuineness of your faith- more precious than gold that perishes, though it is tested by fire- may be found to result in praise and glory and honor at the revelation of Jesus Christ. Though you have not seen Him, you love Him. Though you do not now see Him, you believe in Him and rejoice with joy that is inexpressible and filled with glory." 1:6 ESV

***"Therefore, preparing your minds for action, and being sober-minded, set your hope fully on the grace that will be brought to you at the revelation of Jesus Christ. As obedient children, do not be conformed to the passions of your former ignorance, but as He who called you is holy, you also be holy in your conduct." 1:13 ESV

"Therefore gird up the loins of your mind, be sober, and rest your hope fully on the grace that is to be brought to you at the revelation of Jesus Christ; as obedient children, not conforming yourselves to the former lusts, as in your ignorance; but as He who called you is holy, you also be holy in all your conduct." 1:13 NKJV

*"Having purified your souls by your obedience to the truth for a sincere brotherly love, love one another earnestly from a pure heart, since you have been born again, not of perishable seed but of imperishable, through the living and abiding word of God; for "all flesh is like grass, and all its glory like the flower of grass. The grass withers, and the flower falls, but the word of the Lord remains forever." And this word is the good news that was preached to you." 1:22 ESV

"Since you have purified your souls in obeying the truth through the Spirit in sincere love of the brethren, love one another fervently with a pure heart, having been born again, not of corruptible seed but incorruptible, through the word of God which lives and abides forever." 1:22 NKJV

*"Therefore, laying aside all malice, all deceit, hypocrisy, envy, and all evil speaking, as newborn babes, desire the pure milk of the word, that you may grow thereby, if indeed you have tasted that the Lord is gracious." 2:1 NKJV

*"As you come to Him, a living stone rejected by men but in the sight of God chosen and precious, you yourselves like living stones are being built up as a spiritual house, to be a holy priesthood." 2:4 ESV

"Coming to Him as to a living stone, rejected indeed by men, but chosen by God and precious, you also, as living stones, are being built up a spiritual house, a holy priesthood, to offer up spiritual sacrifices acceptable to God through Jesus Christ." 2:4 NKJV

*"But you are a chosen race, a royal priesthood, a holy nation, a people for His own possession, that you may proclaim the excellencies of Him who called you out of darkness into His marvelous light. Once you were not a people, but now you are God's people; once you had not received mercy, but now you have received mercy." 2:9 ESV

"But you are a chosen generation, a royal priesthood, a holy nation, His own special people, that you may proclaim the praises of Him who called you out of darkness into His marvelous light; who once were not a people but are now the people of God, who had not obtained mercy but now have obtained mercy." 2:9 NKJV

*"Beloved, I urge you as sojourners and exiles to abstain from the passions of the flesh, which wage war against your soul. Keep your conduct

among the gentiles honorable, so that when they speak against you as evildoers, they may see your good deeds and glorify God on the day of visitation." 2:11 ESV

"Beloved, I beg you as sojourners and pilgrims, abstain from fleshly lusts which war against the soul, having your conduct honorable among the gentiles." 2:11 NKJV

*"For this is the will of God, that by doing good you should put to silence the ignorance of foolish people. Live as people who are free, not using your freedom as a cover-up for evil, but living as servants of God. Honor everyone. Love the brotherhood. Fear God. Honor the emperor. Servants, be subject to your masters with all respect, not only to the good and gentle but also to the unjust." 2:15 ESV

"For this is the will of God, that by doing good you may put to silence the ignorance of foolish men- as free, yet not using liberty as a cloak for vice, but as bondservants of God. Honor all people. Love the brotherhood. Fear God. Honor the king." 2:15 NKJV

***"When He was reviled, He did not revile in return; when He suffered, He did not threaten, but continued entrusting Himself to Him who judges justly. He Himself bore our sins in His body on the tree, that we might die to sin and live to righteousness. By His wounds you have been healed. For you were straying like sheep, but have now returned to the Shepherd and Overseer of your souls." 2:23 ESV

"For to this you were called, because Christ also suffered for us, leaving us an example, that you should follow His steps: "Who committed no sin, Nor was deceit found in His mouth"; who, when He was reviled, did not revile in return; when He suffered, He did not threaten, but committed Himself to Him you judges righteously; who Himself bore our sins in His own body on the tree, that we, having died to sins, might live for righteousness- by whose stripes you were healed. For you were like sheep going astray, but have now returned to the Shepherd and Overseer of your souls." 2:21 NKJV

-This is very powerful! Praise Jesus!!

*"but let your adorning be the hidden person of the heart with the imperishable beauty of a gentle and quiet spirit, which in God's sight is very precious." 3:4 ESV

*"Finally, all of you, have unity of mind, sympathy, brotherly love, a tender heart, and a humble mind." 3:8 ESV

*"For whoever desires to love life and see good days, let him keep his tongue from evil and his lips from speaking deceit; let him turn away from evil and do good; let him speak peace and pursue it. For the eyes of the Lord are on the righteous, and His ears are open to their prayer. But the face of the Lord is against those who do evil." 3:10 ESV

"Finally, all of you be of one mind, having compassion for one another; love as brothers, be tenderhearted, be courteous; not returning evil for evil or reviling for reviling, but on the contrary blessing, knowing that you were called to this, that you may inherit a blessing. For he who would love life and see good days, let him refrain his tongue from evil, and his lips from speaking deceit. Let him turn away from evil and do good; let him speak peace and pursue it. For the eyes of the Lord are on the righteous, and His ears are open to their prayers; but the face of the Lord is against those who do evil. And who is he who will harm you if you become followers of what is good? But even if you should suffer for righteousness sake, you are blessed. And do not be afraid of their threats, nor be troubled. But sanctify the Lord God in your hearts, and always be ready to give a defense to everyone who asks you a reason for the hope that is in you."
3:8 NKJV

***"Now who is there to harm you if you are zealous for what is good? But even if you should suffer for righteousness sake, you will be blessed. Have no fear of them, nor be troubled, but in your hearts honor Christ the Lord as holy, always being prepared to make a defense to anyone who asks you for a reason for the hope that is in you; yet do it with gentleness and respect, having a good conscience." 3:13 ESV

"And who is he who will harm you if you become followers of what is good? But even if you should suffer for righteousness' sake, you are blessed. And do not be afraid of their threats, nor be troubled. But sanctify the Lord God in your hearts, and always be ready to give a defense to everyone who asks you for a reason for the hope that is in you, with meekness and fear; having a good conscience." 3:13 NKJV

*"Jesus Christ, who has gone into heaven and is at the right hand of God, angels and authorities and powers having been made subject to Him." 3:22 NKJV

*"that he no longer should live the rest of his time in the flesh for the lusts of men, but for the will of God." 4:2 NKJV

*"The end of all things is at hand; therefore, be self-controlled and sober-minded for the sake of your prayers. Above all keep loving one another earnestly, since love covers a multitude of sins. Show hospitality to one another without grumbling." 4:7 ESV

"But the end of all things is at hand; therefore, be serious and watchful in your prayers. And above all things have fervent love for one another, for love will cover a multitude of sins. Be hospitable to one another without grumbling." 4:7 NKJV

*"Beloved, do not be surprised at the fiery trial when it comes upon you to test you, as though something strange were happening to you. But rejoice insofar as you share Christ's sufferings, that you also may rejoice and be glad when His glory is revealed. If you are insulted for the name of Christ, you are blessed, because the Spirit of glory and of God rests upon you." 4:12 ESV

"Beloved, do not think it strange concerning the fiery trial which is to try you, as though some strange thing happened to you; but rejoice to the extent that you partake of Christ's sufferings, that when His glory is revealed, you may also be glad with exceeding joy. If you are reproached for the name of Christ, blessed are you, for the Spirit of glory and of God rests upon you." 4:12 NKJV

*"Likewise, you who are younger, be subject to the elders. Clothe yourselves, all of you, with humility toward one another, for God opposes the proud but gives grace to the humble. Humble yourselves, therefore, under the mighty hand of God so that at the proper time He may exalt you, casting all your anxieties on Him, because He cares for you. Be sober-minded; be watchful. Your adversary the devil prowls around like a roaring lion. Resist him, firm in your faith, knowing that the same kinds of suffering are being experienced by your brotherhood throughout the world. And after you have suffered a little while, the God of all grace, who has called you to His eternal glory in Christ, will Himself restore, confirm, strengthen, and establish you." 5:5 ESV

"Likewise, you younger people, submit yourselves to your elders. Yes, all of you be submissive to one another, and be clothed with humility, for God resists the proud, but gives grace to the humble. Therefore, humble yourselves under the mighty hand of God, that He may exalt you in due time, casting all your care upon Him, for He cares for you. Be sober, be vigilant; because your adversary the devil walks about like a roaring lion. Resist him, steadfast in the faith, knowing that the same sufferings are experienced by your brotherhood in the world. But may the God of all grace, who called us to His eternal glory by Christ Jesus, after you have suffered a while, perfect, establish, strengthen, and settle you. To Him be the glory and dominion forever and ever. Amen." 5:5 NKJV

2 Peter

*"May grace and peace be multiplied to you in the knowledge of God and of Jesus our Lord. His divine power has granted to us all things that pertain to life and godliness, through the knowledge of Him who called us to His own glory and excellence." 1:2 ESV

"Grace and peace be multiplied to you in the knowledge of God and of Jesus our Lord, as His divine power has given to us all things that pertain to life and godliness, through the knowledge of Him who called us by glory and virtue, by which have been given to us exceedingly great and precious promises, that through these you may be partakers of the divine nature, having escaped the corruption that is in the world through lust." 1:2 NKJV

***"... make every effort to supplement your faith with virtue, and virtue with knowledge, and knowledge with self-control, and self-control with steadfastness, and steadfastness with godliness, and godliness with brotherly affection, and brotherly affection with love. For if these qualities are yours and are increasing, they keep you from being ineffective or unfruitful in the knowledge of our Lord Jesus Christ." 1:5 ESV

"... giving all diligence, add to your faith virtue, to virtue knowledge, to knowledge self-control, to self-control perseverance, to perseverance godliness, to godliness brotherly kindness, to brotherly kindness love. For if these things are yours and abound, you will be neither barren nor unfruitful in the knowledge of our Lord Jesus Christ." 1:5 NKJV

*"And we have the prophetic word more fully confirmed, to which you will do well to pay attention as to a lamp shining in a dark place, until the day dawns and the morning star rises in your hearts." 1:19 ESV

*"But do not overlook this one fact, beloved, that with the Lord one day is a thousand years, and a thousand years one day. The Lord is not slow to fulfill His promise as some count slowness, but is patient toward you, not wishing that any should perish, but that all should reach repentance." 3:8 ESV

"The Lord is not slack concerning His promise, as some count slackness, but is longsuffering toward us, not willing that any should perish but that all should come to repentance." 3:9 NKJV

*"Therefore, beloved, since you are waiting for these, be diligent to be found by Him without spot or blemish, and at peace." 3:14 ESV

"Therefore, beloved, looking forward to these things, be diligent to be found by Him in peace, without spot and blameless; and consider that the longsuffering of our Lord is salvation." 3:14 NKJV

*"You therefore, beloved, knowing this beforehand, take care that you are not carried away with the error of lawless people and lose your own stability. But grow in the grace and knowledge of our Lord and Savior Jesus Christ." 3:17 ESV

"You therefore, beloved, since you know this beforehand, beware lest you also fall from your own steadfastness, being led away with the error of the wicked; but grow in the grace and knowledge of our Lord and Savior Jesus Christ." 3:17 NKJV

1 John

*"that which we have seen and heard we proclaim also to you, so that you too may have fellowship with us; and indeed our fellowship is with the Father and with His Son Jesus Christ." 1:3 ESV

"that which we have seen and heard we declare to you, that you also may have fellowship with us; and truly our fellowship is with the Father and with His Son Jesus Christ. And these things we write to you that your joy may be full. This is the message which we have heard from Him and declare to you, that God is light and in Him is no darkness at all. If we say we have fellowship with Him, and walk in darkness, we lie and do not practice the truth. But if we walk in the light as He is in the light, we have fellowship with one another, and the blood of Jesus Christ His Son cleanses us from all sin." 1:3 NKJV

*"If we confess our sins, He is faithful and just to forgive us our sins and to cleanse us from all unrighteousness." 1:9 ESV

*"My little children, I am writing these things to you so that you may not sin. But if anyone does sin, we have an advocate with the Father, Jesus Christ the righteous. He is the propitiation for our sins, and not for ours only but also for the sins of the whole world. And by this we know that we have come to know Him, if we keep His commandments... but whoever keeps His word, in him truly the love of God is perfected. By this we may know that we are in Him: whoever says he abides in Him ought to walk in the same way in which He walked." 2:1 ESV

***"Whoever loves his brother abides in the light, and in him there is no cause for stumbling." 2:10 ESV

"He who loves his brother abides in the light, and there is no cause for stumbling in him." 2:10 NKJV

*"I write to you, fathers, because you know Him who is from the beginning. I write to you, young men, because you are strong, and the word of God abides in you, and you have overcome the evil one." 2:14 ESV

"I have written to you, fathers, because you have known Him who is from the beginning. I have written to you, young men, because you are strong, and the word of God abides in you, and you have overcome the wicked one." 2:14 NKJV

*"And the world is passing away along with its desires, but whoever does the will of God abides forever." 2:17 ESV

"For all that is in the world- the lust of the flesh, the lust of the eyes, and the pride of life- is not of the Father but is of the world. And the world is passing away, and the lust of it; but he who does the will of God abides forever." 2:16 NKJV

*"No one who denies the Son has the Father. Whoever confesses the Son has the Father also." 2:23 ESV

*"But the anointing that you received from Him abides in you, and you have no need that anyone should teach you. But as His anointing teaches you about everything, and is true, and is no lie- just as it has taught you, abide in Him." 2:27 ESV

*"And now, little children, abide in Him, so that when He appears, we may have confidence and not shrink from Him in shame at His coming. If you know that He is righteous, you may be sure that everyone who

practices righteousness has been born of Him. See what kind of love the Father has given to us, that we should be called children of God; and so, we are." 2:28 ESV

****"And everyone who thus hopes in Him purifies himself as he is pure." 3:3 ESV

*"You know that He appeared in order to take away sins, and in Him there is no sin." 3:5 ESV

*"Whoever makes a practice of sinning is of the devil, for the devil has been sinning from the beginning. The reason the Son of God appeared was to destroy the works of the devil. No one born of God makes a practice of sinning, for God's seed abides in him, and he cannot keep on sinning because he has been born of God." 3:8 ESV

"He who sins is of the devil, for the devil has sinned from the beginning. For this purpose, the Son of God was manifested, that He might destroy the works of the devil. Whoever has been born of God does not sin, for His seed remains in him; and he cannot sin, because he has been born of God." 3:8 NKJV

*"Do not be surprised, brothers, that the world hates you. We know that we have passed out of death into life, because we love the brothers." 3:13 ESV

****"By this we know love, that He laid down His life for us, and we ought to lay down our lives for the brothers. But if anyone has the world's goods and sees his brother in need, yet closes his heart against him, how does God's love abide in him? Little children, let us not love in word or talk but in deed and truth. By this we shall know that we are of the truth and reassure our heart before Him; for whenever our heart condemns us, God is greater than our heart, and He knows everything. Beloved, if our heart does not condemn us, we have confidence before God; and whatever we ask we receive from Him, because we keep His commandments and do what pleases Him. And this is His commandment, that we believe in the name of His Son Jesus Christ and love one another, just as He has commanded us. Whoever keeps His commandments abides in God, and God in him. And by this we know that He abides in us, by the Spirit whom He has given us." 3:16 ESV

*"For if your heart condemns us, God is greater than our heart, and knows all things. Beloved, if our heart does not condemn us, we have confidence toward God. And whatever we ask we receive from Him, because we keep His commandments and do those things that are pleasing

in His sight. And this is His commandment: that we should believe on the name of His Son Jesus Christ and love one another, as He gave us commandment. Now he who keeps His commandments abides in Him, and He in him. And by this we know that He abides in us, by the Spirit whom He has given us." 3:20 NKJV

*"By this you know the Spirit of God: every spirit that confesses that Jesus Christ has come in the flesh is from God, and every spirit that does not confess Jesus is not from God." 4:2 ESV

*"Little children, you are from God and have overcome them, for He who is in you is greater than He who is in the world." 4:4 ESV

"You are of God, little children, and have overcome them, because He who is in you is greater than he who is in the world." 4:4 NKJV

*"Beloved, let us love one another, for love is from God, and whoever loves has been born of God and knows God." 4:7 ESV

*"In this the love of God was made manifest among us, that God sent His only Son into the world, so that we might live through Him." 4:9 ESV

"In this the love of God was manifested toward us, that God sent His only begotten Son into the world, that we might live through Him. In this is love, not that we loved God, but that He loved us and sent His Son to be the propitiation for our sins. Beloved, if God so loved us, we also ought to love one another." 4:9 NKJV

*"Whoever confesses that Jesus is the Son of God, God abides in him, and he in God." 4:15 ESV

"Whoever confesses that Jesus is the Son of God, God abides in him, and he in God. And we have known and believed the love that God has for us. God is love, and he who abides in love abides in God, and God in him." 4:15 NKJV

*"There is no fear in love, but perfect love casts out fear." 4:18 ESV

*"And this commandment we have from Him: whoever loves God must also love his brother." 4:21 ESV

*"For this is the love of God, that we keep His commandments. And His commandments are not burdensome. For everyone who has been born of God overcomes the world. And this is the victory that has overcome the world- our faith." 5:3 ESV

"By this we know that we love the children on God, when we love God and keep His commandments. For this is the love of God, that we keep

His commandments. And His commandments are not burdensome. For whatever is born of God overcomes the world. And this is the victory that has overcome the world- our faith." 5:2 NKJV

*"Whoever has the Son has life; whoever does not have the Son of God does not have life." 5:12 ESV

*"And this is the confidence that we have toward Him, that if we ask anything according to His will, he hears us." 5:14 ESV

*"We know that everyone who has been born of God does not keep on sinning, but he who was born of God protects him." 5:18 ESV

"We know that whoever is born of God does not sin; but he who has been born of God keeps himself, and the wicked one does not touch him. We know that we are of God, and the whole world lies under the sway of the wicked one. And we know that the Son of God has come and has given us an understanding, that we may know Him who is true; and we are in Him who is true, in His Son Jesus Christ. This is the true God and eternal life." 5:18 NKJV

2 John

*"because of the truth which abides in us and will be with us forever: grace, mercy, and peace will be with you from God the Father and from the Lord Jesus Christ, the Son of the Father, in truth and love." 1:2 NKJV

*"...not as though I were writing you a new commandment, but the one we have had from the beginning- that we love one another. And this is love, that we walk according to His commandments; this is the commandment, just as you have heard from the beginning, so that you should walk in it. For many deceivers have gone out into the world, those who do not confess the coming of Jesus Christ in the flesh." 1:5 ESV

3 John

*"Beloved, I pray that all may go well with you and that you may be in good health, as it goes well with your soul... I have no greater joy than to hear that my children are walking in the truth." 1:2 ESV

"Beloved, I pray that you may prosper in all things and be in health, just as your soul prospers. For I rejoiced greatly when brethren came and testified of the truth that is in you, just as you walk in the truth. I have no greater joy than to hear that my children walk in truth." 1:2 NKJV

*"Therefore, we ought to support people like these, that we may be fellow workers for the truth." 1:8 ESV

"We therefore ought to receive such, that we may become fellow workers for the truth." 1:8 NKJV

*"Beloved, do not imitate evil but imitate good. Whoever does good is from God; whoever does evil has not seen God." 1:11 ESV

Jude

*"To those who are called, beloved in God the Father and kept for Jesus Christ: May mercy, peace, and love be multiplied to you." 1 ESV

*"To those who are called, sanctified by God the Father, and preserved in Jesus Christ: Mercy, peace, and love be multiplied to you." 1 NKJV

*"But you, beloved, building yourselves up in your most holy faith and praying in the Holy Spirit, keep yourselves in the love of God, waiting for the mercy of our Lord Jesus Christ that leads to eternal life. And have mercy on those who doubt; save others by snatching them out of the fire." 1:20 ESV

*"Now to Him who is able to keep you from stumbling and to present you blameless before the presence of His glory with great joy, to the only God, our Savior, through Jesus Christ our Lord, be glory, majesty, dominion, and authority, before all time and now and forever. Amen." 1:24 ESV

Revelation

*"and from Jesus Christ, the faithful witness, the firstborn from the dead, and the ruler over the kings of the earth. To Him who loved us and washed us from our sins in His own blood, and has made us kings and priests to His God and Father, to Him be glory and dominion forever and ever. Amen." 1:5 NKJV

*"I, John, your brother and partner in the tribulation and the kingdom and the patient endurance that are in Jesus." 1:9 ESV

*"I know you are enduring patiently and bearing up for My name's sake, and you have not grown weary. But I have this against you, that you have abandoned the love you had at first. Remember therefore from where you have fallen; repent, and do the works you did at first." 2:3 ESV

"and you have persevered and have patience, and have labored for My name's sake and have not become weary." 2:3 NKJV

*"Do not fear what you are about to suffer. Behold, the devil is about to throw some of you into prison, that you may be tested, and for ten days you will have tribulation. Be faithful unto death, and I will give you the crown of life… The one who conquers will not be hurt by the second death." 2:10 ESV

"Do not fear any of those things which you are about to suffer. Indeed, the devil is about to throw some of you into prison, that you may be tested, and you will have tribulation ten days. Be faithful until death, and I will give you the crown of life." 2:10 NKJV

*"Therefore repent. If not, I will come to you soon and war against them with the sword of My mouth. He who has an ear, let him hear what the Spirit says to the churches. To the one who conquers I will give some of the hidden manna, and I will give Him a white stone, with a new name written on the stone that no one knows except the one who receives it." 2:16 ESV

"Repent, or else I will come to you quickly and will fight against them with the sword of My mouth." 2:16 NKJV

*"... I will give to each of you according to your works." 2:23 ESV

*"The one who conquers and who keeps My works until the end, to him I will give authority over the nations." 2:26 ESV

"And he who overcomes, and keeps My works until the end, to him I will give power over the nations." 2:26 NKJV

*"I know your works. Behold, I have set before you an open door, which no one is able to shut. I know that you have but little power, and yet you have kept My word and have not denied My name." 3:8 ESV

"I know your works. See, I have set before you an open door, and no one can shut it; for you have a little strength, have kept My word, and have not denied My name." 3:8 NKJV

*"Because you have kept My word about patient endurance, I will keep you from the hour of trial that is coming on the whole world, to try those who dwell on the earth. I am coming soon. Hold fast what you have, so that no one may seize your crown." 3:10 ESV

"Because you have kept My command to persevere, I also will keep you from the hour of trial which shall come upon the whole world, to test those who dwell on the earth. Behold, I am coming quickly! Hold fast what you have, that no one may take your crown." 3:10 NKJV

*"And they sang a new song, saying: You are worthy to take the scroll, and to open its seals; for You were slain, and have redeemed us to God by Your blood, out of every tribe and tongue and people and nation, and have made us kings and priests to our God; and we shall reign on the earth." 5:9 NKJV

*"For the Lamb in the midst of the throne will be their shepherd, and He will guide them to springs of living water, and God will wipe away every tear from their eyes." 7:17 ESV

"for the Lamb who is in the midst of the throne will shepherd them and lead them to living fountains of waters. And God will wipe away every tear from their eyes." 7:17 NKJV

*"saying, we give thanks to you, Lord God Almighty, who is and who was, for you have taken your great power and begun to reign. The nations raged, but your wrath came, and the time for the dead to be judged, and for rewarding Your servants, the prophets and saints, and those who fear Your name, both small and great, and for destroying the destroyers of the earth." 11:17 ESV

"saying: We give You thanks, O Lord God Almighty, the One who is and who was and who is to come, because You have taken Your great power and reigned. The nations were angry and Your wrath has come, and the time of the dead, that they should be judged, and that You should reward Your servants the prophets and the saints, and those who fear Your name, small and great, and should destroy those who destroy the earth." 11:17 NKJV

*"And they have conquered him by the blood of the Lamb and by the word of their testimony, for they loved not their lives even unto death." 12:11 ESV

"And they overcame him by the blood of the Lamb and by the word of their testimony, and they did not love their lives to the death." 12:11 NKJV

*"He will wipe away every tear from their eyes, and death shall be no more, neither shall there be mourning, nor crying, nor pain anymore, for the former things have passed away." 21:4 ESV

*"And He said to me, it is done! I am the Alpha and the Omega, the beginning and the end. To the thirsty I will give form the spring of the water of life without payment. The one who conquers will have this heritage, and I will be his God and he will be My son. But as for the cowardly, the faithless, the detestable, as for murderers, the sexually immoral, sorcerers, idolaters, and all liars, their portion will be in the lake that burns with fire and sulfur, which is the second death." 21:6 ESV

"And He said to me, "It is done! I am the Alpha and the Omega, the beginning and the end. I will give of the fountain of the water of life freely to him who thirsts. He who overcomes shall inherit all things, and I will be his God and he shall be My son. But the cowardly, unbelieving, abominable, murderers, sexually immoral, sorcerers, idolaters, and all liars shall have their part in the lake which burns with fire and brimstone, which is the second death." 21:6 NKJV

CRUSHERS

POWERFUL SCRIPTURE

**"I will sprinkle clean water on you, and you shall be clean from all your uncleanness, and from all your idols I will cleanse you. And I will give you a new heart, and a new spirit I will put within you. - And I will put My Spirit within you, and cause you to walk in My statutes and be careful to obey My rules." Ezekiel 36: 25-27

**"Bless the Lord, O my soul; and all that is within me, bless His holy name! Bless the Lord, O my soul, and forget not all His benefits; who forgives all your iniquities, who heals all your diseases, who redeems your life from destruction, who crowns you with loving kindness and tender mercies, who satisfies your mouth with good things, so that your youth is renewed like the eagles. The Lord executes righteousness and justice for all who are oppressed. He made known His ways to Moses, His acts to the children of Israel. The Lord is merciful and gracious, slow to anger, and abounding in mercy. He will not always strive with us, nor will He keep His anger forever. He has not dealt with us according to our sins, nor punished us according to our iniquities. For as the heavens are high above the earth, so great is His mercy to those who fear Him; as far as east is from the west, so far has He removed our transgressions from us. As a father pities His children, so the Lord pities those who fear Him. For He knows our frame; He remembers that we are dust. As for man, his days are like grass; as a flower of the field, so he flourishes. For the wind passes over it, and it is gone, and it is renewed no more. But the mercy of the Lord is from everlasting to everlasting… On those who fear Him, and His righteousness to children's children, to such as to keep His covenant, and to those who remember His commandment to do them. The Lord has established His throne in heaven, and His kingdom rules over all. Bless the Lord, you His angels, who excel in strength, who do His word, heading the voice of His word. Bless the Lord, all you His hosts, you ministers of His, who do His pleasure. Bless the Lord, all His works, in all places of his dominion. Bless the Lord, O my soul." Psalm 103

**"Consider it all joy, brethren, when you encounter various trials, knowing that the testing of your faith produces endurance. And let endurance have its perfect result, so that you may be perfect and complete, lacking in nothing." James 1:2-4

**"Do not lie to one another, since you laid aside the old self with its evil practices, and have put on the new self who is being renewed to a true knowledge according to the image of the One who created him." Colossians 3:9-10

**"And do not be conformed to this world, but be transformed by the renewing of your mind, so that you may prove what the will of God is, that which is good and acceptable and perfect." Romans 12:2

**"The steadfast of mind You will keep in perfect peace, because he trusts in You." Isaiah 26:3

**"For the mind set on the flesh is death, but the mind set on the Spirit is life and peace." Romans 8:6

**"Now. little children, abide in Him, so that when He appears, we may have confidence." 1 John 2:28

**"Love, joy, peace, patience, kindness, goodness, faithfulness, gentleness, self- control." Galatians 5:22

**"But He knows the way I take; when He has tried me, I shall come forth as gold." Job 23:10

**"Most gladly, therefore, I will rather boast about my weaknesses, so that the power of Christ may dwell in me." 2 Corinthians 12:9

**If there is a breakthrough waiting for you because of God's sovereignty, the enemy will put thoughts in your mind to intimidate you and they become a stronghold. He wants to confuse us. God tells us:

"The enemy will come in like a flood, but the Spirit of the Lord will raise up a standard against him." Isaiah 59:19

"The enemy comes to Steal, Kill, and Destroy, but God has come to give us life to the fullest." John 10:10

"Don't be anxious for anything, but in everything, but in everything with prayer and thanksgiving present your requests to the Lord, and the God of peace Will Guard Your Hearts." Philippians 4:6-7

CRUSHER JOURNAL

COLLECTION

---

*Grapes must be crushed to make wine. Diamonds form under pressure. Olives are pressed to release oil. Seeds grow in darkness – whenever you feel crushed, under pressure, pressed, or in darkness, you're in a powerful place of transformation. Trust the process.

*Keep watch and stand like a statue of peace and strength

*Watch over your heart with all diligence. Strong mentality and peace. Fortify yourself and hold strong in faith.

*Just because you are struggling does not mean you are failing.

*Real security can only be found in that which can never be taken away from you; your relationship with God.

*Being strong solves a lot of life's problems

*Choose to fill your mind, imagination, and emotions only with God's power and truth. Your soul will prosper, and when your soul prospers you will prosper in life and be in health.

*Prepare your mind for action and be focused on the light in your heart.

*Spiritual Stone, Steadfast Rock, stand and don't be moved. Do your best to face opposition but do it by giving the situation to God and trusting Him to complete your victory. Confidence thru the fire.

*Work towards the crown of life and the lives of others with understanding and kindness.

*Do not worry or be troubled, do not worry about things you cannot control. Focus on the things you can affect, the things you have control over. Don't overthink.

*Strong and bold, inner peace and strength. Know that sometimes the best way to be strong is to be meek. Happy are the poor of spirit. You don't have to be mighty all the time. You can win the fight in innocence and peace.

*Don't give up - endure to the end - patience - day at a time

*Kindness and gentleness

*Take heart and fortify your mind

*Put on the new self - purity

*In truth there is freedom

*Be upright - Be like a stag in the forest, alert, and like a lion of power and peace

*Peacemakers, instruments of peace, reason, and mercy

*Love and peace in your eyes. Practice fixing your gaze in light and strength. Stay focused on your spirit.

*Sometimes the best response is no response - "Even fools seem smart when they are quiet."

*There is a lesson in everything - "You will have bad times, but they will always wake you up to the stuff you weren't paying attention to."

*"Respond to your children with love in their worst moments, their broken moments, their angry moments, their selfish moments, their frustrated moments, their inconvenient moments because it is in their most unlovable human moments that they most need to feel loved."

*If it is not truth do not let it enter your mind

*Patient endurance is great. Satan attempts that he might bring out the worst in us, but God permits it that He might bring out the best in us.***

***The trials of life are meant to mature us, build our faith, strengthen us, and to get us to trust the Spirit. Of course it hurts to have the experience, but trust in the process that you are being refined and made into something great!

*Tell God exactly how you feel, but also tell Him that you love Him and trust Him always.

*The Spirit can work in your life when your body, mind, and will embrace Him.

*The only way to conquer is to surrender to God and walk like Him.

*Faith it until you make it.

*Courage is resistance to fear, the mastery of fear, not the absence of fear. If you are afraid know that fear drives faith! If you feel afraid try to turn that fear into the fear of God and know that your courage is growing.

*We grow because we struggle. We learn and overcome.

*If you are in a situation that is difficult, take courage and choose how you react to the situation, consistently choose to face the issue positively and in faith.

*Observe your thoughts. Face every thought, and practice self control. Analyze your heart and replace any bad thought with truth and freedom.

*Fix your eyes! Discipline yourself and conduct yourself in the peace of God!

*You have to defeat those feelings that hold you back and learn how to have peace and strength in every situation. Discipline your heart and mind. Correct yourself to do what you should do. Submit your cares to the Lord, you will overcome for you CAN do all things! Life wouldn't be so hard if we didn't expect things to be so easy! You are a soldier who washes feet! Peace

*Mental toughness involves a consistent ability to remain determined, focused, confident, and in control under pressure. Toughness is not an innate thing and more of a learned thing. Fight the good fight.

EDGE OF THE SWORD

Luke 10:26, 11:9, 17:21, 18:1
John 1:4, 12:46, 13:13, 13:34, 15:2, 16:33, 17:18
Acts 2:25, 14:22
Romans 5:1, 6:10, 8:6, 12:9, 16:20
1 Corinthians 16:13
2 Corinthians 1:9, 12:9
Galatians 2:20, 5:1, 5:22, 6:7
Ephesians 3:16, 4:1, 4:23, 4:29, 6:10, 6:14
Philippians 1:6, 2:3, 2:14, 3:12, 4:4, 4:13
Colossians 1:10, 2:6, 3:12
1 Thessalonians 5:8, 5:14
2 Thessalonians 2:2, 3:5
1 Timothy 1:3, 6:11
2 Timothy 2:1, 2:3, 2:15
Hebrews 1:1, 8:10, 12:5, 12:11
James 2:8, 3:2, 4:7
1 Peter 1:13, 2:21, 3:13
2 Peter 1:5
1 John 2:10, 3:3, 3:16

COMPLETE COLLECTION

Matthew:

3:10, 4:16, 5:3, 5:14, 5:37, 5:43, 6:2, 6:8, 6:20, 6:22, 6:24, 6:33, 7:5, 7:7, 7:12, 7:14, 7:15, 7:21, 7:23, 7:24, 9:11, 9:37, 10:7, 10:16, 10:22, 10:32, 10:34, 10:38, 11:29, 12:20, 12:25, 12:37, 13:23, 13:31, 13:37, 13:41, 14:27, 14:31, 16:18, 18:11, 18:15, 18:20, 19:26, 20:26, 21:13, 22:37

Mark:

4:14, 4:20, 4:30, 6:2, 8:34, 9:23, 9:37, 9:39, 9:50, 10:15, 12:10, 12:29-34, 13:7, 13:13, 13:37, 14:38

Luke:

1:17, 1:51, 1:74, 1:77, 2:9, 2:14, 3:8, 3:11, 4:18, 5:31, 6:43, 6:46, 8:15, 8:21, 8:48, 9:50, 9:55, 9:62, 10:2, 10:19, 10:26, 10:37, 11:9, 11:17, 15:10, 17:21, 18:1, 18:17, 20:38

John:

1:4, 1:9, 1:12, 3:3, 3:17, 3:21, 3:36, 4:37, 6:27, 6:29, 6:33, 6:37, 6:45, 6:63, 7:18, 7:37, 8:12, 8:31, 8:34, 8:42, 8:51, 10:9, 12:46, 13:13, 13:20, 13:34, 14:1, 14:6, 14:9, 15:2, 15:8, 15:18, 16:2, 16:20, 16:24, 16:33, 17:3, 17:11, 17:14, 17:18, 17:22, 18:37, 20:31

Acts:

2:21, 2:25, 2:38, 4:11, 5:29, 7:49, 9:31, 10:34, 13:47, 14:22, 16:31, 20:35, 26:17

Romans:

1:9, 1:16, 1:18, 1:21, 2:10, 3:23, 4:7, 5:1, 5:8, 5:20, 6:1, 6:10, 6:16, 6:18, 8:1, 8:6, 8:10, 8:13, 8:18, 8:28, 8:31, 8:37, 10:10, 10:12, 12:2, 12:9, 12:18, 15:13, 16:20

Corinthians 1:

1:30, 2:4, 2:9, 2:12, 3:7, 3:9, 3:11, 4:8, 4:11, 6:9, 6:11, 6:20, 7:32, 9:14, 10:13, 10:23, 13:4, 13:13, 14:12, 14:33, 15:33, 15:42, 15:56, 16:9, 16:13

Corinthians 2:

1:3, 1:9, 2:7, 2:14, 5:14, 5:17, 5:19, 8:7, 9:6, 12:9, 13:3, 13:7, 13:11

Galatians:

1:3, 1:10, 2:20, 5:1, 5:13, 5:16, 5:22, 6:1, 6:7

Ephesians:

1:13, 1:17, 2:1, 2:10, 2:12, 3:12, 3:16, 4:1, 4:23, 4:29, 4:32, 5:7, 5:15, 5:17, 6:10, 6:14

Philippians:

1:6, 1:10, 1:14, 1:21, 2:3, 2:14, 3:12, 4:4, 4:13, 4:19

Colossians:

1:6, 1:10, 1:22, 1:26, 2:2, 2:6, 2:13, 3:12, 3:17, 3:23, 3:25, 4:2, 4:5

1 Thessalonians:

2:4, 2:11, 3:2, 3:12, 4:2, 4:9, 5:4, 5:8, 5:14, 5:21

2 Thessalonians:

2:2, 2:10, 2:16, 3:2, 3:5, 3:7, 3:12

1 Timothy:

1:3, 2:2, 3:16, 4:4, 4:7, 4:12, 4:14, 5:1, 6:6, 6:11, 6:17

2 Timothy:

1:7, 1:9, 2:1, 2:3, 2:11, 2:15, 2:19, 2:21, 2:24, 3:1, 3:12, 3:14, 3:16, 4:5, 4:7, 4:17

Titus:

2:2, 2:11, 3:1, 3:4

Philemon:

1:6, 1:20

Hebrews:

1:1, 2:10, 2:17, 4:14, 5:9, 6:10, 7:19, 7:24, 8:10, 8:13, 10:4, 10:12, 10:16, 10:19, 10:22, 10:24, 10:35, 10:39, 11:6, 12:5, 12:11, 12:14, 12:28, 13:1, 13:3, 13:5, 13:14, 13:18, 13:20

James:

1:2, 1:12, 1:19, 1:21, 2:8, 2:13, 3:2, 3:13, 3:16, 4:3, 4:7, 4:12, 5:8, 5:12, 5:13, 5:15, 5:19

1 Peter:

1:6, 1:13, 1:22, 2:1, 2:4, 2:9, 2:11, 2:15, 2:21, 2:23, 3:4, 3:8, 3:10, 3:13, 3:22, 4:2, 4:7, 4:12, 5:5

2 Peter:

1:2, 1:5, 1:19, 3:8, 3:9, 3:14, 3:17

1 John:

1:3, 1:9, 2:1, 2:10, 2:14, 2:16, 2:17, 2:23, 2:27, 2:28, 3:3, 3:5, 3:8, 3:13, 3:16, 3:20, 4:2, 4:4, 4:7, 4:9, 4:15, 4:18, 4:21, 5:2, 5:3, 5:12, 5:14, 5:18

2 John:

1:2, 1:5

3 John:

1:2, 1:8, 1:11

Jude:

1:1, 1:20, 1:24

Revelation:

1:5, 1:9, 2:3, 2:10, 2:16, 2:23, 2:26, 3:8, 3:10, 5:9, 7:17, 11:17, 12:11, 21:4, 21:6

ABOUT ME

My name is Justin Bolster, I was born in Baltimore, Maryland in December 1984. God raised me and blessed me with a big amazing loving family. I grew up playing outside with brothers, cousins, and friends and exploring nature. I played a lot of sports growing up and had a lot of fun. I never got below a B in middle school but always wanted to fit in with the cool kids. In High School I told my dad that I didn't want to be smart, I wanted to be cool. So, I started skipping school, smoking cigarettes, weed, and drinking on a regular basis. I got a 0.0 GPA one semester because I totally did not care. I basically majorly messed up. I ended up in a mental hospital and got into severe spiritual warfare. So by the time I was 20 I was severely ill. So, I could not give up and have endured over 18 years of hardship. I have listened to many sermons and have read books to grow in Christ and fight for my mind and my life. I am now confident in how amazing our Lord is and can love and praise Him! He is my Lord and Savior always through and through. He has never left me, though I felt lost. PRAISE HIM!! What I do now is continue to fight the fight in my mind, and to have victory all the time. The gospel is truly a great weapon and to understand and abide in truth is amazing! I pray that Jesus will open your eyes and heart to be light in this world. There is truly nothing to fear and everything to live for. LOVE and be intimate with the heart of Jesus and reflect it all day. You are free indeed! We walk as lions! Peace everybody! Blessings!! – Jus

--This book was created for the last days, today, and always. Designed to equip each soldier with all the truth needed to achieve victory and receive salvation. Understand it, practice it, and don't give up. Peace always!

Printed in the United States
by Baker & Taylor Publisher Services